THE BILLION DOLLAR CHANNEL METHOD

The Real Estate Agents YouTube Roadmap

JACKSON WILKEY

info@channeljunkies.com

First Printing, May 2023

Book cover design by ebooklaunch.com

ISBN 979-8-3960-4007-6 (hardcover)
ISBN 979-8-3960-3705-2 (paperback)

www.channeljunkies.com

Contents

Preface

In the words of a famous genius "The definition of insanity is doing the same thing over and over and expecting less-shitty results." Ok, I'm paraphrasing a little, but you catch my drift.

Have *you* had enough of cold-calling, pounding pavement, and selling your soul for something that generally gives a pretty bad return on your investment?

Well, it's time to put down the rotary phone and that ancient Rolodex because there's a better way to get you more clients, more dough and better work/life balance than you could've ever imagined.

In this book, I'll show you exactly how we have used YouTube to make $6.4M in gross commissions and consistently close 3 deals per week over the past 36 months. And yes, this method also continues to work for you during a recession.

This book is your ultimate guide to leveraging YouTube to attract clients and become the most popular agent in your area. With the power of these simple techniques, you'll be selling properties faster than you can say "I fucking love money."

Now, I know what you're thinking: "But I don't have the time or equipment to make videos!" No worries, I've got you covered. I'll show you how to create amazing content with just your smartphone and I'll show you how to get started right away.

So get ready to learn how to be the YouTube agent you never knew you could be. This book will change the game for your real estate business and have you laughing all the way to the bank. Let's do this!

CHAPTER 1

How We Got Here

"If it comes easy it's not worth it. If it's worth it, it won't come easy."

– *Anonymous*

As I sat, ears ringing from the silence of what felt like a million failed phone calls, I couldn't help but wonder if I'd made a huge mistake.

Had I *really* just plunged my family into debt, given up the highest paying job in our hometown, and moved us all away from everything and everyone we knew... for nothing? Would I be back soon, tail between my legs, carrying a giant serving of humble pie? Nope. I don't give up that easily, particularly when it affects my family. But, you know, the doubt seems to have a way of creeping in when stuff isn't going your way. Since we started this thing, I've second-guessed myself so many times, but there have also been these incredible moments when all the pushing made sense.

This story certainly doesn't follow the usual straight line that every other successful real estate "guru" spins. Nope, that shit was brutal and I'm more than prepared to be honest with you about that.

See, this journey starts because it was never supposed to happen in the first place. 327 closings in less than 3 years, $174M in sales, clients reaching out to us *who actually want to work with us*, helping thousands of agents learn how to YouTube; that shit never should have happened.

To learn how I got the fire to keep pushing through without being the best agent–and after a hundred videos that didn't work even after spending tens of thousands of dollars on marketing–you need to know how it all began.

Now, while I'd love to tell you that this is a rags to riches story, the truth is that I was making amazing money in my hometown of Coeur d'Alene, Idaho. I'd grown up there, my best buds were there, and I was currently holding down the highest paying job you could get in this town. As a journeyman lineman, I had the toughest job you could get, they only had like one opening every 5 years.

From the outside, I had everything; loving family [√], good friends [√], badass boat [√], and enough cash to not worry. A $100k-a-year salary is not a number to sniff at in most any community, but in Coeur d'Alene, I was one Rich Bitch. Roll on Monday morning, however, and my stomach would churn at another day of to-the-minute being told what to do and when to take my lunch break.

To give you a little background: Coeur d'Alene is a logging and mining town, with no real economy or corporate structure outside of that. It's basically a breeding ground for blue-collar work. That's it. Growing up, you're not taught entrepreneurship or anything useful outside of the town. You're just basically there to get through school, find a career job, and work until you retire or die–whichever comes first.

If you look at the Coeur d'Alene housing market today, most people born and raised there are not able to afford a house because it's a right-to-work state and the market has fully outgrown that rule. A lot of my friends are making 10, 11, 12, or 15 bucks an hour. And with this crazy-ass housing market, property prices have completely surpassed.

So I'm working this job, and it's Union. You can't show up one minute late. You can't leave one minute early. I mean it's literally like a cartoon where they punch the clock in, punch the clock out in a neverending cycle. We showed up at the exact same time every day, and we did the exact same thing every morning. We were absolute creatures of habit. Now, we made a lot of money. Well, according to the folks of Idaho, but being told what to do, where to be, and how to do it *every single day* was just miserable.

I'd show up to work, people would tell me what to do. I'd eat lunch when they told me to eat lunch, and we'd eat that crap in a dirty-ass work truck. I was always either cold, hot, or dirty, and I knew that I had to go back to that grind again the next day.

I'll never forget this one day when I was on my boat, on stunning Hayden Lake, which was just a couple minutes from my house. I had a triple toon pontoon boat and a slip on the lake. Like, that's the life. On the weekends, you get to enjoy it all and you're just like, "yep, I've made it." At the sandbar hanging out drinking brewski's, what's not to love? I was making way more money than anyone else there, and I had a boat, a wife, two kids, and a beautiful house on a golf course.

But man, come Sunday, the clock would strike 12:01 p.m. and this gnawing feeling would start creeping up in my gut, like it was trying to warn me that something was seriously not right with this picture. But like just about anyone thinking about upending their life would do, I began to browbeat myself, "Why are you feeling like this, Jackson? You have everything." Even my work buddies would be like, "Jackson, what's your deal? It's not that bad." They were all content to work their 35 to 45 years, retire, and then deal with a laundry list of health issues. I mean, even at that point, we were a walking surgery room.

Roll-on Monday morning and I would be seething with frustration and anger, because I knew that the same routine was about to start right back up again. I'd wake up at 4:30 in the morning, before the kids even got up, and I'd already be in a foul mood. All that boating fun from the weekend would vanish as if it never happened, and everything would start to irritate me. Meanwhile, my buddies who didn't have jobs like mine would be sleeping in until at least 6 in the morning. My wife and kids would be having a blast while I was already miserable. It was just the worst feeling, and it really put a strain on my relationship with my family. Something had to give.

So after five long years of being a journeyman lineman, I knew I had to make a change. That's where my desire to succeed with video and YouTube for real estate comes from, and you gotta hear the backstory to understand why I was never giving up and why you shouldn't either.

CHAPTER 2

How to Be Yourself on Video

I still remember my buddies, Conor and Garett, leaving North Idaho for bigger things. Conor was a genius and went to Princeton, then ended up in New York as an investment banker, raking in the dough. I always saw his pictures, he would post them on Facebook and send them in texts every once in a while. I was like, "God, I'd die to do that." Meanwhile, my best friend in the whole world, Garett Jerde, went to the University of North Dakota with five of our other friends to become pilots. All but Garett became pilots. He went straight into selling jets, and eventually made his way to Dubai where he started his own business and became a millionaire. Everytime he would come back to town, he would walk into the bar, order a hundred shots of Patrón, and everybody knew Dirty Jerde was here.

I just kept seeing the lives of my friends who moved away, and created this new story for themselves. They were making money AND enjoying life. So I asked around them, with super subtle hints like "you should give me a job." They all responded with something along the lines of, "no dude, I mean, I can't help you." So I started reaching out locally.

Now, I knew everybody in this town. I was one of the top athletes to ever come out of there, ranked as one of the top five basketball players in Idaho history. I played college ball locally, and I was just a nice dude. So I hit up every single person I knew, trying to find a new spot. The first lead I got was with a huge flooring company. I knew a sales rep there who was making $150,000 a year. This guy was bringing in more money than I was, and he was doing it by slanging carpet. He says to me "Jackson, I'm about to retire. You know, I could probably get you in." I'll never forget how pumped I was thinking I had a definite shoo-in. However, I never heard a word back from him.

Then, the Hayden Lake Country Club had a kind of a summer general manager role, and I knew the guy who was running the whole show. Working there meant that I could also be around influential people who might be able to give me more direction. I said to the head dude "I would love to do this. Just get me around these people." He replies with "Jackson, this is not for you man. Like, this is like a 30-40k a-year job." I come back with "I don't give a shit. Let me do it." He wasn't having it, he knew I'd be outta there faster than a street-legal golf cart. Well, that job also turned out to be dead in the water.

Around this time my wife's childhood bestie, Pearl Bay, and her husband Zach were coming to visit us from Portland. Zach and Pearl had left South Idaho years ago. He'd been in banking and escrow forever, and was recruited by WFG National Title to work as an escrow title officer. This guy was making money hand over fist and having fun doing it.

So, Zach comes to hang out with us on our boat and, being the stand-up human being he is, pretty quickly notices the struggles I'm having with my job. As we cracked open a couple cold brewski's, Zach looks at me and says, "Dude, you would kill it in sales." I nodded, telling him I'd been trying to break in for a while. "I bet I could get you a job as a sales rep for escrow," he continued, "These guys make a killing. Some of them are making 200, 300, 400 grand a year."

I nearly choked on my beer. "You're shitting me," I said.

"Nope," he replied, smiling. "I can hook you up."

We made a plan for me to head to Portland to meet with the Marketing Director of WFG National title, the company Zach was working for. This guy knew the ins and outs of the sales biz and was happy to help me out and introduce me to the sales manager. We meet. We do a shit load of shots, drinking, and hanging. Being from a small town in Idaho, I can hold my own. Next we head over to the Marketing Director's house. He invites over another guy who was a sales rep for First American Title. So, we're continuing on the booze train, slinging those brewski's back like they're going out of style, and the guys are like "you're going to *crush* sales dude." I'm not going to lie, that felt good to hear. They also suggested that I work for First American Title instead of WFG National Title so that they could actually pay me some decent cash from the get-go.

As I arrived home from my trip to Portland, I was feeling pretty good about myself. I had just aced the first meeting with the title company guys, and was confident that I'd impressed them enough to land a job. Before I left, they had said they'd be reaching out to me soon, so I'm at work thinking "I'm getting out of here." So I just coasted, completely unaware that I was about to embark on the longest, most brutal half-a-year of my life.

So, 6 months go by and not a word. And at this point, I'm thinking "well, that dream is over too." It felt like every door I tried opening closed right in my face. But just when I was about to give up, I got the call I had been waiting for "Jackson, can you come down for an interview?" Hell yes I could.

I fly into PDX, and get to this interview. I'm sitting there with the title company people dressed to the nines. They start interviewing me about marketing and inquiring about my sales history. Now, I grew up working on a ranch and at this particular moment in time I'm a journeyman lineman, working on power lines. I do have a Bachelor's degree in Communications, so I can talk that talk. That's it though–I was interviewing for a job I had zero experience in. They're basically going off the recommendation from my friend Zach.

The Marketing Director of WFG National Title and I had also become homies (still are to this day), so he put in a good word as well. When I left that interview, I wasn't feeling super confident that they'd even *consider* hiring me. So, I go back and sit for a little bit, waiting for some kind of verdict. Eventually they approach and say "hey, we know you're traveling home and we don't want you to wait... We don't have all the financials worked out yet, but we're going to hire you." What?! I couldn't believe it, finally I was getting traction. They continued, "why don't you head home and we'll give you a call to let you know what the pay scales are and all that." I am jacked-up at this; this sense of going from Union labor worker and missing all my kids birthdays to a whole new gig where I could potentially be making bank.

During that moment, I remembered a time when there was a crazy storm in Idaho. It went on for two weeks straight, with six feet of snow. It was a proper freeze. We had no power, and we had our six-month-old daughter wrapped up in eight layers. She was breathing steam out of her mouth while sleeping that night. But with this new opportunity, I realized we wouldn't have to do that anymore. I felt like getting into sales would open us up to a normal life. I was so fucking excited. I couldn't wait to get home to tell my wife.

I get home and a couple of days pass. Killing time and getting ready for our new transition, my wife and I cruise over to Spokane, Washington, which is about

30 minutes to the west of Coeur d'Alene, to do a little shopping. At this point, I know I'm getting hired, it's just how much. We're both happy about the prospect, but I'll never forget, we're in downtown Spokane and we're about to head into one of my wife's favorite stores and the phone rings. It's the Marketing Director of WFG National Title, the guy I'd done *all* the shots with in Portland. I turn to my wife and say "Honey, here it is." I'm smiling ear-to-ear. This is the call. This is what I've been waiting for.

"What's up Jackson?"

"Yeah, man, how's it going?"

"Well, we're ready to hire you and I got the numbers right here. So, what we're looking at is a salary of $42,000 a year."

"Oh, shit." I think.

Now, I know that I was previously willing to take that job at Hayden Country Club for <$40k, but this offer was quite a bit lower than I thought it'd be.

He continues, "But, obviously, it's sales. So, you know, you'll be able to work up."

My wife breaks down into tears. She is bawling her fucking eyes out. I cannot. It's painful to replay it in my mind. I knew she was devastated. You might be thinking, "oh, yeah, it's because you're not making as much money." Nope, she'd built a very successful massage business in our town. Her clients loved her, she had her dream schedule, and she made great money. She adored what she did, and she had built her own business from the ground up. When the call came in, reality hit and she knew that we'd be leaving all that behind. And now her man is making $40,000 a year instead of $110,000. Not just that, it's *way* more expensive to live in Portland. Yet, I wanted something that wouldn't strain our marriage, a new path where we could both be happy and make each other happy for years to come. Even with everything that was going on, I'm a half-glass full guy and I'm immediately saying, "yeah, honey, but I will go kill it. That's just the starting pay. I'll work up, I will make this money back. It's all good, we got this shit." I believed all that, but that didn't stop it scaring the shit out of me. As we drove home that night, the car fell quiet and the conversation ran dry while we both processed what had just happened.

In the end, I took the job. We talked about it and I promised her that it'd open doors and get us to a better setup for the future. Now, my wife's a badass. I've had some of the craziest ideas in my life and she's always been my ride or die. I can't thank her enough for all of the chances she's been willing to take together. Also, one of the saving graces was that her best friend, Pearl, who I mentioned earlier, was living in Portland. That helped but it still meant that we'd be moving from North Idaho and away from everything we'd ever known. I knew every street, every road, house, bar owner, shop owner, fishing hole, and every hunting spot. All the things that can make a person feel secure. And now I'm going to an area that's full of liberals and crazy-ass Portlandia people. But, honestly, I didn't care, we just needed that opportunity. So towards the end of 2017, my oldest son, Hank, *a.k.a Hank the Tank*, and I head to Portland, Oregon, ahead of the rest of the family. We're going to go stay with Zach and Pearl. My wife and my daughter, who was about a year old at the time, stayed back to pack up. They were planning on staying home for about a year. The reason I was taking my oldest son was because we could get him into school right away. Which if you have kids, you'll know that timing is everything.

Before we hit the road, I had to break the news to my family members and my buddies. Thing is, you just don't leave North Idaho. Some friends got it, but I also had a few friends who truly snubbed the shit out of me. "You'll be back," they said before continuing to drive the blade further between the shoulder blades with "You'll fail," and "Portland's a shithole." Now I'm moving, uprooting my entire family, and half the people I'd spent my life with didn't even believe in me. It's a pretty shitty feeling to say the least, but when it came down to the wire, I didn't care–I would do anything to not be a lineman anymore. So, we hightailed the hell out of there, and about 6 and a half hours later (give or take a few pit stops) we arrived in Portland. After just a few months, my amazing wife and awesome baby girl showed up. That made it official: Portland, Oregon, was our new way of life.

I will never forget the first day that I sat down with our Chief Marketing Officer at WFG. On that day, it felt like I was sitting in a foreign language class. No-one there spoke any kind of anything that I could understand. I came from Idaho, building power lines; grew up as a ranch hand, I was nothing short of a Keystone-guzzlin' redneck. I didn't even have social media when I lived in Coeur d'Alene. So I sat there, trying to understand what on earth he was saying.

This guy spoke to me like I knew the game, I knew real estate, I knew what agents needed. But I was so damn lost. There must have been a ten-minute period where I think I was looking straight through him or out the window, and I don't remember a single word this man said. I'm a very optimistic guy, but I had no idea about all these marketing platforms, computer programs, transaction management, and CRMs. The only thing I knew that was close to CRMs was a CR250, a Honda dirt bike.

On one of the days that followed, the company's owner comes in. The CEO. This dude is 75 years old, but great looking for 75. Shorter dude, I mean, he's like barely up to my tit. He had huge bushy hair, one of those kind of chiseled jawlines and his face stretched down tight to it, beady eyes, dressed to the nines; this dude was scary as shit. He walks in and basically just starts laying into the sales team, basically telling them that they need to get their shit together. And he starts kind of role-playing, *clearly relying on what he used to do back in the 1910s*, to show the reps how to be as successful as he is today. So brosef is lecturing us to ensure we're getting in our ten calls a day. I remember a couple of sales reps even managed to get a word in edgeways by giving excuses as to why they couldn't make their calls, and he wasn't having that. His undoubtedly incredible action plan for us was to pick up the phone and dial ten calls a day. And the guy made sure that he went through what we should be doing on these calls and what our value propositions were. It was kill-me-now-and-don't-look-back kinda terrible.

I remember thinking, Oh, my God, what did I get myself into? I already knew that I hated bugging people. I couldn't make a cold call to save my life. I could not prospect these agents, even though I tried. Now I would sit in my office, and they would give me these scripts and value propositions to regurgitate out to these agents, who were already receiving way more of these calls than they'd like. We'd get these momentous packets of phone numbers to call. These things had so many lines of contacts on them that you'd have to trace each line with your finger so not to lose your place.

Now, the reason I was hired was that my market center where I was had about 42% market share. We dominated over there, and our considerably ancient leader wanted more of that. But what this entailed for me was going into all the shittiest offices, that had very low production, or offices where we'd already *artfully* burned the bridge. These agents seriously do not like our title company. Along with the behemoth list I mentioned a moment ago, we were given a list of the top 20 agents in our area. Every sales rep had a top 20 list to go after, and the first 5 deals you got from it would land you with an oh-so-sweet $1,000 per deal. I was making 40 grand in a year, so that golden list meant a shitload of money for me. I was cold calling these people–trying every tactic I could think of. I'd pace around my office and try to build myself up, and practice these god-awful scripts.

"Hey, is this [insert random agent's name here]."

"Yeah, who's this?"

"Hey, it's Jackson, your title rep here at WFG National title."

And then from there, I'd freeze solid and forget my words. Was it because I didn't believe in the plastic and completely insincere words that had been sprawled out before us? Or was it just nerves in general? Probably a bit of both, but I spent at least half my time at that company scrambling for the sheet that bore this atrocious scriptwriting. It was brutal. Of course when I was calling that many people in a day, I did land a couple of appointments, and it was usually with newer agents who didn't have a title company yet. That got me in the door a few times, but as I started really progressing into this sales career, I realized that I might be able to offer these people something different than other reps. Something that didn't eat away at my soul either. A couple of months into it, the one thing that I was hearing, no matter what class I went to; no matter what brokerage I walked into; no matter what agent, was that they all wanted to get better at their marketing, and every single one of them was talking about video. The video was all the rage.

So this is 2018. It's not like the video was brand new. iPhones, killer video cameras, there are tons of programs for editing, there's YouTube, there's Facebook, there's Instagram. It wasn't brand new, but every single real estate agent I talked to, kept bringing up video.

I had this thought one day, and I'll never forget it. I was in my tiny-ass condo with my unimaginably awesome wife, and I looked at her and said, "I've figured it out. I'm going to start shooting a bunch of videos for real estate agents about how they can shoot and edit their own videos. Honey, I'm going to go from lineman to in-man. That's going to be the story." She's like, "that's actually a pretty cool thing." Now, neither she nor I knew what an in-man was before all this, but by the time we had this conversation, I knew that an in-man was like a marketing guru. And with that statement, I had my own unique sales proposition. So I went onto eBay, and I bought a 2012 MacBook Air for $235. My beautiful niece has that computer to this day. That computer is how I got my start, and I'd like to thank Steve Jobs for also never giving up.

Next thing to do was to come up with a brand. Since my last name is Wilkey, I came up with Wilkey's Wisdom. Yep, looking back now I know that the name could've used some work from the get-go, but if you've seen the original Amazon website, you'll know that we all have to start somewhere. Not only that, but I got this banner made. This magnificent piece of history had none other than The Rock standing in front of a cloud of smoke, donning his infamous lifted brow. It was pure class, to say the absolute least.

I began shooting videos to send to all of these real estate agents. They would be the videos that got said agents reaching out to work together. And that's the beauty of our current system–you don't spend hours of your day calling people who don't want to be called by you. Instead, you're getting qualified people who have already seen you, they already trust you, and they're amped to get started right away. It's magic.

As mentioned, I started out knowing nothing about any of this, but within four to six months, I was pretty well-versed in Facebook, Instagram, Google My Business, and now the much in-demand video. It went from that to obsessing over data analytics, Facebook ad campaigns, split-testing, retargeting, and that is truly where I began to separate myself from the other reps. It was the beginning of a whole new path and the reason I'm writing this book to you today.

To think that just a few years ago, I was staying in my wife's best friend's basement, broke as a fucking joke, and now we're sitting on millions? Yeah, it feels even better than it sounds.

CHAPTER 3

This Never Should've Happened

Meeting Jesse Dau! The craziest thing about it is it was, it never should've happened. And boy did I get a wrath of shit from this girl who was nuttier than squirrel turds. She was a sales rep in one of the other offices who really didn't want me to have any business at all–but more on her later.

So here's how Meeting Mr J Dau went down: One day I get a life-changing phone call from Mr. Zach bay. He's the one, if you remember, who came to my house in Idaho, my wife's best friend's husband. He's the one who got me to Portland and gave us a place to stay when we got there. Zach's one of the top; if not the top, escrow officers in all of Portland. Everybody wants him. He's the GOAT. To this day, I love him to death.

Zach was doing me solids left and right. Any deals that crossed his desk and weren't already assigned, he passed onto me. Tbh, I was living with his ass and he was probably trying to make me more money so I could get tf out of his house. One day, he hits me up and he says, "Hey, I got this guy who just submitted to title his new listing, and he is not attached to anybody. It's a million-dollar listing. You should give him a call." And I'm like, "Hell. Yes." He sends me over the information, and it's none other than Mr Jesse Dau. At the time, I didn't know the guy, so I obviously started by first doing a little creeping (everybody does it—don't pretend you haven't). Once I land on Jesse's Facebook, I dig in. This stranger's first pictures were of him sitting on his doorstep, with his wife at the time, and two Labradoodles. Scrolled a little and he seemed like a decent enough dude, so I made the call. Ring, ring... it's his voicemail, "Hi, this is Jesse Dau with NextHome Realty Connection." Like, in a really high pitch. I'm sitting there thinking, "oh boy." I leave a message with the mind that I'd follow up in a few days.

I don't remember the exact words I proclaimed to his voicemail that day, but it went something like, "Hey, it's Jackson Wilkey with WFG National Title. I saw you put in your listing with us, and I'm gonna be helping you out. I see it's a million-dollar listing. Just wondering if you want me to help you with some of your marketing efforts to get this listing out there to as many people as possible. Give me a call back when you get this."

At this point, I've been in the game for about five to six months. I had already started leveraging social media marketing. This was back in 2017 or 2018, when listings sat on the market for 60 days and luxury listings sat for months. So, getting as many eyeballs on this listing as quickly as possible was super important. I knew how to run targeted Facebook ads to hit some of the wealthier areas where people were moving and looking to buy million dollar homes.

A week went by and I decided to try a different tactic to get this dude's attention. I had recently found this app called InShot video. In this app, you can record yourself in video format and then add all these emojis. It's kinda like Snapchat, with a ton of useful filters and overlays. The way I used it was to drop in some kind of emoji for almost every sentence that I spoke. I left Jesse a second message, this time sending the video I'd just made. In this thing I've got emojis and all this crazy popping up all across the screen. I send it over to Jesse, and nothing happens. Roughly three days later, he calls me and says, "Hey man, you know, I saw your video, and everything, and yeah let's meet up man. I'd love to learn more about how we can market this listing, this luxury listing." I'm like, "holy shit, it worked." I couldn't believe it. I'd later learn that this was the first time anybody ever reached out to him with a video at all, much less one with tons of shit flying everywhere.

I just knew that whenever I sent these InShot videos to other agents, they'd typically respond back with, 'Oh my gosh, I love that video. It was so funny. How do you do that? I'd love to start doing that for my clients." Jesse took it as like, "Hey, I've never been reached out to in that way. It was very personal. Like, okay, this guy means business." And if you know Jesse, he means business alright. He doesn't waste his time. His biggest kicker in life is *do not waste his time.*

So Jesse invites me over to his brokerage, which was Next Home Realty. I walked through the door and I'm thinking that this is one of the coolest micro brokerages I've ever seen. I had been going into all the conglomerates as well as a bunch of little offices, but this was a super cool open-air space. It had a modern vibe with this big garage door that would lift open to the street. I look over to my left, and there are a couple of beer taps, and I'm thinking, "Yeah. This place is epic."

That day, I had my cowboy boots on. I won't forget that. I think he looked at me like, "Well, this is different." And he's from Oregon City, which is a small town itself. The fact it was the ending point for the Oregon Trail kinda goes to show how small-town it is. So, we instantly had that in common. Our first conversation started as, "Dude, this is actually really cool in here. Did you guys remodel this?" And he's like, "Yeah, man. I mean we did a bunch of remodeling and made it nice." I said, "Sweet, dude. I actually gut and flip houses and do a lot of remodeling. I've done flooring just like this." And Jesse goes, "Dude, me too. I actually did a huge remodel on a house not so long ago."

It wasn't until later that I'd realize just how much meeting Jesse would change my life. We talked for over an hour about remodels. I was currently remodeling the house that we bought. And he's like, "I got a contractor's account, where you can go in and get a bunch of your stuff 20% off." He generously gave that info to me and I ended up getting my flooring there–with a sweet discount. Even though, realistically, we were polar opposites, Jesse and I hit it off from the get-go.

So, we get started on his million-dollar listing by running Facebook ads. It was then that we started to get attention from one particular person who I'd rather avoid. The sales rep I mentioned at the beginning of this chapter. I was, apparently, stepping on her turf. If I was ever within a square mile of one of her clients, she would call to bitch me out. Super pleasant person. And what made it worse was that she would have this totally bubbly personality with everyone else. So she calls me, like she always did whenever she felt like I was encroaching on her territory, and I'm thinking "not today, Satan." I pick up and she starts bashing me out right away, "That's my client. What are you doing?" I respond with, "Well, Zach gave him to me." So then she gifted Zach with her stellar personality. But Zach didn't take the bait, he made it clear that he'd given it to me because I was physically closest to it. The office I was working out of was way closer to the listing than she was. Jesse being who he is, once he trusts you, he will fight for you. So, I put her on speakerphone so he could hear the shit she was talking to me. At the sound of it, he went into ultra-defense mode and set her straight. And I'm thinking that maybe that adversity brought us closer together all that much faster.

Jesse and I had been talking for a while, and I got to telling him about these killer ribs I thoroughly enjoy making... I mean, falls right off the bone, you can eat a whole rack without noticing, makes-you-wonder-if-they're-even-legal kinda ribs. Jesse had seen a few videos I made while smoking some up and asked me if I'd make some for a Broker Open he was having to get eyes on another lux mansion he had listed. Hmm, let's see... Bbq and brokers AND a possible luxury mansion deal? Yeah I was in, but I was also completely broke. "Hell yeah, just pay for the ribs," I say. So, Jesse rolls up with a giant 3-pack of ribs and I smoked them up. It was fun, it made it felt like shit was actually starting to happen.

After that, Jesse and I just kind of started forming this real bond. We talked every day, sometimes multiple times a day. With everything I'd pushed through and for, it was an awesome feeling to know someone like Jesse had my back. Being new to sales and still trying to get my feet wet, I all of a sudden had someone who was already doing a lot of production, that I could just talk to.

For Jesse, even though he was relatively new to real estate, he already had a successful business that was doing 12 million in volume. What he had accomplished in such a short period of time was practically unheard of. But Jesse being Jesse, he wanted to strive for more. He had his mind set on building a real estate media and marketing company. But he didn't really know what that looked like. Meanwhile, I had been hitting up every other agent in Portland, offering to shoot and edit videos for them free-of-charge. All they had to do was show up, but none did, except Jesse. He'd always be there, and he didn't care what videos we shot. He just wanted to get started. Jesse's a well-decorated, killer agent and he had the knowledge I needed in order to progress. I had the knowledge he needed. So, naturally, we decided to team up and take this business to the next level.

Right around the same time as all of this is going on, I sign up with a popular online Facebook marketing guru. I realized that sales reps in the company I'd been working for, and other companies, weren't going out of their way to learn social media tactics. Many agents *use* Facebook ads but they don't always know how to use them properly. So building knowledge about social media marketing for real estate was my gateway into working with more agents and making a living while Jesse and I planned on building our online empire.

But Jesse had doubts. He was like, "Dude, this is not a market that Facebook ads work in. Portland is more expensive." Yes, I get that Facebook ads killed it in the Phoenix Arizonas of the nation. Sure, Phoenix can be pretty spendy, but it was also littered with $150,000 to $200,000 homes. And you could run these ads and get these cheap deals all day long. And that's what people were doing. But Jesse was right, Portland was more expensive, it just wasn't the right crowd. Still, I said, "No, dude, I'm in these groups. These people are converting. Even if we convert 1%, I can get these leads down to a dollar or 50 cents. I can get us a thousand, dude. If we close 1% of that, you know, we're talking 10 deals a month." Jesse thinks about it before responding with "All right, man, I'll fund it."

So I'm a sales rep for escrow and he's doing real estate. I'm running his Facebook ads and now I've got it so dialed that I'm running campaigns with some pretty complex funnels. Viewers would see a video, and if they watched it for X amount of time, they would go down one of the eight funnels we had set up. We would work them down these funnels to where they saw all of Jesse's branding, including all of his past client reviews. We literally bombarded the Portland Metro with these Facebook ads. In my mind, it was a gold mine and we worked those leads. Well, not 'we,' I didn't, but Jesse did. Eventually Jesse comes to me and says, "Man, they're just shit leads. Like these clients can't afford anything." And I'm like, "I know, but it takes a little bit of time. We gotta convert." So I'm basically meeting with him every day, running his Facebook ads and shooting videos with him and this is the path we take for the next few months.

Now, I'm working in escrow and starting to make at least a little bit more money. My wife, who had built a popular massage business in Idaho, also started in escrow after having to leave her business behind. She had become an escrow assistant. That was the worst time of her life. So, I had this brilliant idea: my wife should get licensed in real estate! I'd run the ads, she'd convert them. That was the idea.

And, since I'm just going to keep it 100% with you guys throughout this book and tell you the truth, the main reason I wanted her to get licensed and work those deals was because I *hated* these Facebook leads. I loved building the systems but I could not stand anything else about it. I'd seen and heard the discussions Jesse had with some of these Facebook leads and it was atrocious. I wanted to run as far away from it as possible, but I also wanted to get paid on it.

So, now I'm going to force my wife to do something I would hate to do. Like I said, brilliant idea. Still, she goes online and starts doing her schoolwork. She's getting a bit done here and a bit done there. I remember saying to her, "Why aren't you doing that?" But why was I doing that? Why was I trying to force the love of my life to do something she absolutely doesn't want to do and has no passion about.

Looking back on that now I'm like, "man, what a jerk!" Worse still, I didn't even have my license yet. I wasn't being fair. No matter what crazy idea I've had, my wife has supported me. When I wanted to become a journeyman lineman, I had to go to a school that cost us $9,000 and *also* not make money for four months. She said, "Go, do it." You know, I think a lot of times in relationships, people have their own goals and they don't support their partner because they're zeroed in on what *they* want to achieve. That beautiful, caring woman has supported me more than any human ever, so I stopped pushing her to this thing that she obviously despised.

One day, Jesse and I are sitting there talking, he looks at me, and says in a very sensible tone, "What are you doing? You gotta get licensed, man." I respond to him with a knowing look, "I've really been thinking about it." Jesse continues, "You're never gonna make money doing what you're doing. You've gotta get over on this side." And that's all it took. I'd been a sales rep for 11 months and was turning heads, but I knew that path would just lead me to, once again, working for someone else.

Now, as you know, it takes a little bit to get your license. But my foot was out the door the minute Jesse reminded me that if I wanted to level up, I had to take another sizable risk. I'd made it this far and wasn't giving up now. I knew I had to work fast. I still remember, during the last few weeks of my tenure as a sales rep, I spent every day in the empty little library in the city. Nobody goes there, but I hid in the corner of this tiny place while I studied, because I actually thought a sales rep or manager would catch me. I went and I studied my ass off all day long–while I was still on the clock. Within two weeks, I had all of the work done and was ready to test.

When the day of the test rolls around, I'm pumped. However, I also had a title rep sales meeting that morning for work. The meeting ends at 10 and the test is at 2, so I've got time. I'm in this morning meeting and they're talking about all this new stuff and all these flashy things, but I'm just not interested anymore. Instead of listening, I'm going by memory and studying for the real estate test. The sales meeting ends and I remember thinking to myself, "okay, my test is at like

2:00 or 3:00 PM. Right now, it's 10 in the morning. Screw it, I'll just drive to the parking lot just to make sure I'm not late and I'll study. From 10ish to noon, that's what I did. But, you know, you can only spend so long sitting in your car and intensive studying has its limits too. I decide to walk in and ask if they have space ahead of my time slot. Happily, they did.

You know there's that saying 'if you don't ask, you don't get'? Well, that's my mindset a lot of the time. What's the worst thing that can happen if you just do the damn thing and ask? People say no. And as I'm sure you're aware, you tend to get a lot of no's in real estate. So in a way, my test began the moment I asked them that question.

"Yeah, we got plenty of room," they respond, "Just go ahead and sign in."

At this point, my heart is racing. Am I making a mistake? Am I going to pass this test? Will I make any money at all? Will my family and I be even *more* broke? Was that even possible? We've all been there when the doubt starts creeping in. But in order to get anywhere in life, you've got to ignore that inner dialogue. So I sit down, take the test, pass, and I get my freaking real estate license.

CHAPTER 4

First 6-Month Ass Kicking

So, here I am with this new real estate license. But before I get into the excruciating next few months, I got to tell you about the cheesiest-ass video that I've ever made: Holding my phone on a selfie stick and strolling around Jesse's office space, which had just become my new office space, I started, "*It's a beautiful day in Portland and especially here at Next Home Realty connection...*" It goes on and it was one cringe-worthy moment, to say the least. Still, I put out this Facebook Live video. The only problem was, up until this point, I had been a title sales rep. That meant that I'd spent all of my time in Portland building relationships with real estate agents, not potential buyers or sellers.

I'd spent the last eleven months of my life getting to know every real estate agent I possibly could in the community. I had a few friends and neighbors, but that was about it. Rough start, but the video got the ball rolling in a different way than expected. After seeing the novice video, not one but two top real estate agents called me. I had still kept my cards pretty close to my chest about becoming an agent, but the post had exposed me. They called me hot, 'Jackson, hey, come sit down with me, please.'

The first of these two dudes, Drew, was one of the first real estate agents that I'd met when I moved to Portland, Oregon. I'd met him after going to a party at the house of my title company sales manager. There were a few real estate agents there and one of them ended up being this dude. Now I thought I was tall, but this guy's like 6"7'. I'm 6"3', so I was definitely looking up to him. On that day, I didn't know who the hell he was. I was not aware of the major accomplishments he's made in the real estate game. But there was a mini dunk hoop in the backyard of the house where the party was being held. I'm a Hooper–I love hoops. So, this dude and I were kind of shooting around. I'm in my dress shoes, it's like my first week of work. Even so, I take off and dunk on this eight-foot hoop. Drew looks and goes, "You played, haven't you?" Thinking back to the days where I was one of the best semi-pro players in my hometown, I said, "Oh yeah, man. I love hoops." With an interested look, he continues "We run every Monday, Wednesday, Friday, and Saturday mornings at 05:00 a.m." Well, the day I met him was a Friday, and he had just invited me to join them the following day.

"You're going to show up tomorrow?" He says. And I'm like, "Oh, yeah." He goes, "You're not showing up!" Don't tell me not to do something, or don't tell me I can't do something. So right there, I said, "Hell yeah,

I'm showing up." With a look of doubt on his face, he says, "Yeah, we'll see." So, I ended up going and playing that morning.

I'm a high-energy dude, I fly around, and your boy's got bunnies. At least I used to. Once I hit about 33, or 34, they're pretty well gone. But in college, I was a 45-46" vertical guy. So I'm there, and this guy could see that I could play a little bit. He and I end up just talking and hitting it off. That's when I learn that he's the third highest grossing real estate agent in all of Portland. And I think at the time I'm writing this, he's probably close to number two or number one. He was already giving his business to WFG. So I was getting nothing from that. But throughout my whole tenure there in Portland, there weren't many Mondays, Wednesdays, or Fridays that I missed. And that was kind of my escape.

I loved waking up in the morning, and I remember that was usually the time that I was waking up and getting ready to go work power lines. And now I get to go play basketball and shower, get the kids ready for school. So, Drew and I really created this tight bond. But Jesse and I had made this relationship throughout the last four/ five/ six months to where it was a no-brainer. Like, I was partnering up with this kid. He's a killer. He's got a vision, right? Drew wanted me to be a part of his team. He just saw my personality and how good I was with people. He knew I would be good, and he wanted me on his team.

He was one of the first real estate agents that I met when I moved to Portland, and the third highest grossing agents in the city. The second had been one of my top 20 agents when I was a title sales rep.

Even though I spent a few mornings each week playing basketball with the first dude and had worked extensively with the second, I'd also recently been sitting shoulder to shoulder with this dude Jesse every day. Well, not shoulder to shoulder, he's about a foot shorter. They all had impressive sales sheets, but Jesse had a similar vision to mine. That's when I really started buckling down with Jesse.

At our office, we had a gal who sold a lot of new construction, and they were nice homes. I would go sit in these homes every single day. You know the deal; when potential clients would walk in and give that look of like, *oh, shit, there's the agent, there's the used car salesman, he's going to bombard me*, that really threw me off my game. It made me feel pretty shitty. As time went on, I was finding it harder and harder to spark up conversations with these people. I was no closer.

Jesse, however, is a *killer* closer. This dude spent 15 years in two of the most impressive sales and training companies that corporate America had to offer. He knows his shit. In those previous roles, he had become very comfortable with scripting and role-playing. He knew that it was a method that worked. I thought that was the most awkward thing in the world, but it was just so easy for him. It's just how he's wired. For me, it was my biggest nightmare. And honestly, it's why I never closed people at open houses–I didn't put in the work to get good.

I would listen to these top-selling agents all the time. In fact, I met this guy who had won Rookie of the Year at Keller Williams, and he crushed it with open houses. So I called him, "Dude, I know we're both in real estate now, but how do you crush the open houses?" He gave me his scripts. The more I learned about how he got deals, and the more I learned about Jesse and how he got deals, pushed me deeper and deeper into this depression. No matter what I did, I couldn;t bring myself to do the things you have to do to be a closer. I started resenting the fact that I had to go to open houses.

At this time, I had two kids, so they're starting to do things and extracurricular activities on the weekends, and I'm missing it. Sometimes on the weekends, I'd sit there thinking "God, I hope people just don't even show up so I can wrap this damn thing up." All I wanted to do is be around my kids, and I'm sitting there in an open house that felt more like the opening to hell. At the same time, I carried this weight, and maybe you felt it, too, that you're letting people down. Not just my wife and my kids. In my mind, I was going through these motions to impress Jesse with my client-getting skills. Like, this dude was pouring a lot of time and energy into me and helping me out. If I wasn't going out, prospecting and ultimately closing these clients, then I was letting my family and Jesse down. I felt it every day.

It got to a point early on when I'd just go through the motions, to show Jesse that I was doing the busy work. To this day, I don't think I've ever really talked to him about that. Chasing the client was something that I dreaded, and deep down I knew that it just wasn't going to happen for me. But when you're making absolutely no money and you're in brand new territory, you have to do the work. So I kept doing it, and I did start practicing what to say and what to do at these open houses. As they walked through the houses, I'd ask prospective buyers "So, what's got you in the area?" Just to get some kind of conversation going. I swear to God, the only people that I had great conversations with, and we totally hit it off, already had an agent.

The next aspect was cold calling. Jesse had gotten the majority of his business from cold calling and open houses. He was damn good at it. So, we'd practice our scripts, and work on cold calling, and to me it was the worst thing on planet Earth. I hated it.

One day he says, "You know what? I'm already paying my coach. He's the number one cold caller in the country. I'll just get you access to his cold calling course." So I'm like, "All right, perfect." So I log in, and look through every single script. I print them out and start practicing... It was easier for me to practice alone with nobody around because I found cold calling so awkward. After that, I was starting to feel a little more confident. But when objections would truly hit, your boy would go running. I hung up on so many people.

Jesse even had this robo dialer. I would log into this thing, and there were all these brand new FSBOs and expired listings. I would start going down the list and calling them, *praying that they wouldn't answer.* After about a month of doing this, and hearing whispers of this "DNC" list, I thought I'd best be checkin' about what the latter was. "What's that?" inquiring about this mystery list. I was informed that, legally, I wasn't supposed to call these people. So, I went back and looked at all the lists of people I had called. Sure enough, 90% of them were on this list. Oops.

Eventually, I landed my very first listing appointment. I couldn't believe it–these people finally accepted me AND were going to let me into their house. So I go over to this house, and it's a three-bedroom, two-and-a-half bath condo townhouse, almost identical to the one that I was living in at the time. My whole listing presentation to them was about drone videos and the ability to target hundreds of thousands of eyeballs with Facebook ads.

Now, Jesse always told me our fee was 6% for anyone we worked with. We don't take shortcuts and we don't bring on tire kickers. As I'm sitting at this listing appointment and Jesse's in the back of my mind 'okay, 6%, show them what you're worth.' They come back with "Well, we really like you. Would you be willing to do it for 4.5%?" And I said, "Well, I only do 6%, because you've got to realize that we need to market this property. I'm going to get it to tens of thousands of eyeballs that other agents just can't. They do not know how to leverage social media." With that, I pulled up my laptop and showed them how I could create their ads for them. They really loved that. This is back in 2018, probably early 2019, during the housing market slowdown. You had to really work to get an offer on a house.

I had decided that I was worth it and I wasn't leaving that place without a contract or 6%. Well, I left that place with neither of them. But they did say they were going to call me and let me know. To seal the deal, I wedged a handwritten note in the crack of their door, just appreciating them for their time, and reiterating how hard I'd work for them. It took a minute, but they texted me, *"Thank you for the note. We really appreciate that Jackson, but we decided to go with another agent."* So I reached out and said, "Well, thanks for the opportunity, but where did it go wrong?" They said, "Oh, she just chose to do it for 4.5%." Now I had to go tell Jesse I didn't get this listing. I said, "Yeah, dude, because the agent they chose did it for 4.5%." He goes, "Well, why didn't you do it for 4.5%? Why wouldn't you?" A little confused about my prior training, I said, "You always said 6%." "Well, yeah, but you need to negotiate and adjust it. You got to get the listing," he says.

Through the wonder of mailers, I finally did get a listing. It's just rough real estate marketing, but it worked better than anything else I'd tried.

Every day, I'd walk down to the end of our road with my son and get him aboard his school bus. After doing this for many months, I became super tight with some of the other neighborhood dads. We'd meet down there every morning and chill long after the bus had left.

This one awesome day, my neighbor says, "Jackson, I got your mailer the other day, and I just wanted to ask you something; I'm going to be selling my house, and I was wondering if you would do it, but do it for a discount." And I'm like, okay, we know what happened the last time I stuck to my guns at 6%. So in my mind, I'm thinking, "Okay, hell yeah, I'll do it. Whatever you want." He asks for my card. This was the moment, but I couldn't even breathe. I can't get words out of my mouth. I'm stumbling. I'm shaking. And even though Portland spends most of its year on the cooler side, I'm probably sweating *profusely.* I'd not had a deal in six to seven months, period. No money. Getting my ass kicked every single day, and someone comes up and asks me to sell their house *all from a mailer.* I sprinted home as fast as I could. I said, "Wait right here." I grabbed my business card, gave it to him, and I said, "Yes. Why don't we just schedule a time, and I'll come by?" He said, "Perfect. I got your card. I'm going to email you when we're free."

I go home and call Jesse, freaking out. He says, "Let's get you prepared, man. Let's role play." Fuck, not that again. Urgh. It's not just that, everything about real estate stresses me out. Nevertheless, I get this script printed out. We painstakingly thumbed through this script, page after bles-sed page. And the end of this, Jesse turns to me and proclaims, "Lock this fucker down. You got this shit."

The last thing that Jesse told me before I went into this presentation was, "Hey, he wants you to do it for cheap. You go through this whole entire listing plan, and at the end of it, you look him right in the eyes, and you say, 'now, if I do all of this for you, am I still only worth 1.5% to you or am I worth more like 4?'"

I get to my neighbor's house and run him through the listing presentation. At the end of it, I say to him in a very direct tone, "Now, after seeing this whole entire marketing plan and everything that I'm going to do for you; with the drone, the videos, custom pictures, and running Facebook ads, do you still think that I am only worth 1.5%? Because we typically charge 6." That was it, I had nailed it. I sounded just like Jesse. The guy then looks back at me with a quizzical and kinda miffed look on his face. He returns my words with, "No, I'll just call somebody else. You said you'd do it for 4%. If you're not going to do that, I'm not using you." Not letting this deal slip out of my hands, I say, "Perfect. Let's sign it." I was not going home without that damn listing, and 4% was better than 0%. They signed on *the line which is dotted* and we were in business. That was my big break, I thought, I was finally starting down the road to unforetold riches.

Getting into the office, I tell Jesse. He was pretty proud of me. He said, "Alright, well, let's knock it out of the park." He goes, "On what price did you settle?" Not wanting to say it out loud but knowing I had to tell him that I'd agreed to sell this house for ten grand more than top market value; "Oh, yeah, well, he said he'll only sell it at $320,000." A little shocked, Jesse turns around and says, "Jesus Christ, what the hell did you do in there?!" "Look, I had to get the listing. He wanted top dollar. He wanted 4%. I just figured you're the best in the business, Jesse. You'll get this shit." He's like, "Okay, man, what is wrong with you?" Damn, I knew what he was saying but wasn't giving up on it, "I don't know, man, but let's just do it."

So we create a killer listing video including drone footage and a mini vlog of the area. I even put my kids in it; swinging, showing this crazy cool park that was right by our house. All the shops, restaurants, bars, all of the key places you'd want to see before moving to an area. Then we get the professional pictures out. We're doing all this stuff. The market at the time was tougher than usual, but we actually started getting people very quickly. The open houses were hot and heavy. I knew we had done absolutely everything we could.

The offers started rolling in. The seller wanted $320,000. It comped out at $310,000 maximum. We finally get this lady who obviously wanted this house so freaking bad. She was coming in just $6k below the 320 marker. "Jesse, what do you think?" Without even taking a split-second to think about it, Jesse replies, "Oh, dude, I'm telling you right now, an offer of $314,000? You've got to get them to accept that. There's no possible way we can get any higher than that at all, period. Just get them to accept it. Tell them it's the best offer. It's clean." So I call the seller up.

This is back when offers above the asking price were still fairly rare. I'm hoping that the seller has changed his mind... "No, we only want 320." Urgh. I tried to bring it home by letting him know that we'd probably be on the market a lot longer, and that would lead us to a place where we'd most certainly only get under asking. "No, not taking it," he says. "Go back at them and tell them we're only accepting 320." Oh goddamn it. We're working ten times harder than Jesse and I ever did on any other listing, and we're making ten times less than we should.

I return to Jesse and tell him, "Dude, he's not accepting it." Stifled, Jesse says, "You've got to be fucking kidding me." "Alright," he continued, "you need to call that buyer's agent. You need to tell her, 'hey, we love the offer, but my clients are only accepting 320. We have four other written offers in hand, so if your client wants to lock it down today, that's what they need to come in at." I did, and the agent responds with some pretty damn great news, "I think she'll do it," She says, "Thanks for talking with us."

The offer comes back at 319 as the max they'll do. I tell my clients and also point out that there would be a month of rent back, so it would actually work out to be a hair above 320. "Perfect. I knew you could do it," the client responds, "We'll take that." Hell. Yes. The first deal in contract, I think agents can take themselves back to that first one and remember what a great feeling it was to close. I'm making a $1500 paycheck, but it was a huge win.

Right around that time, I'm going on the first vacation we'd taken since landing in Portland. We'd planned this thing a year in advance, and it just happened to land right when I had my first listing. Obviously, Jesse knows about the vacation plans. But we were at the point where everything was getting scheduled, inspections and all that. I don't quite remember what it was, but something fell through on the deal. We were in Mexico, and so I'm trying to relay all this information to Jesse.

Jesse gets on the phone and I'm thinking 'oh shit, here goes our entire business because I've let him down AND he's doing all the work at the moment', "Damn It, Jackson. Next time you leave, you give me your clients' cell phone, email, wife, husband, all the information, and every document you have when you go on fucking vacation. If you go on vacation, you don't work. I will take care of it. That's what partnerships are for." In my mind, I was thinking, 'Oh. My. God. That's the nicest thing that anyone's ever said.' I couldn't believe he said it. Instead of just handing me my ass, he did the exact opposite. "You're on vacation with your family. That's what you should be doing, not dealing with this." So he *was* mad, but he was mad that I didn't give him all the information beforehand.

So, I gave him all the information. Within 3 hours, it was back on track and he got it to the closing table. He's a gangster. I do not have the ability to do that. Having those tough conversations with those clients was the hardest thing in the world for me. It's not for Jesse. He walks right and tells you right to your face. I'd known that he was a better real estate agent than me, but now I got to see that shit in action. My business partner was a Killer.

CHAPTER 5

The Bailout

Burnout in real estate is all too common. According to the National Association of Real Estate, 87% agents leave the profession within 5 years. Other statistics suggest that up to 80% drop out around 2 years in. 26% make over $100k a year while just 10% make over $200k a year. The national average income? Just $46,340. And, given the way the economy is, you'd be lucky to get a decent burger for that price in a few years. I'm not saying this to depress you, just to give you the facts about the situation. And is it really a surprise? You bust your ass off to try and get deals, and then bust it again to close said deals. All while trying to work with people who don't always want to work with you. That's a recipe for disaster. Yep, in our fair profession burnout is real.

According to statistics, and the fact you're reading this book, you're either starting to feel the burnout or could be at some point. Before Jesse and I really started to double down on YouTube, we were both at the verge of burnout. He was a top agent, but that also meant that he was working 20 hours a day at one point. 20 HOURS A DAY! The man is a machine, but no machine can keep going without proper maintenance and a guy's got to sleep at some point.

We cold called, robo-dialed, held open houses and talked to people who didn't want to talk with us. We went so far above and beyond for our clients, and honestly, got paid like shit in comparison to the damage it was doing to our private lives, health and sanity.

One day it just hit me, was this really what real estate is like? You go way and above and beyond for these clients, and they're going to pay you nothing. Some see the imbalance and feel bad about it. They'll say that you did so well that they'll refer their wealthy aunt and every passing stranger to you. But then life goes on and you never hear from them again. I felt like people were just using me because I was cheap. For me, real estate was not fun. It wasn't fun at all.

Before YouTube started to take off, I was feeling pretty low about real estate. I'm running these open houses and it's killing me. I eventually started getting better at the open houses. My first decent Open House was this $750,000 house Jesse listed. Back then, $750,000 got you a mansion. Nowadays, that's kind of your middle price. I'll never forget this one day when I was just on fire. I'm shooting videos every day. I'm documenting every single thing that Jesse and I do. I'm shooting community videos. All I could think about all day was just shooting videos. For some reason, in my mind, I thought, if I just keep shooting these, I'm going to start getting reach-outs. So my whole passion was behind the videos, but that was not paying. That's why I still had to continue doing these real estate things. So, it was a rare day where I actually enjoyed doing an open house.

So I'm at this open house, a gorgeous home, and this first set of clients or future clients walkthrough. It's a couple. They're right at my age. I'm 6'3", the husband's probably 6'5", and the wife is probably 6'3". So, we had that in common. Dude was dressed head-to-toe in Nike. I also had my Nike's on at this point and they were Jordan's. So, he and I just hit it off. They were moving to Portland and were both high-up workers in Nike. This house is right down the road from the campus. So I was like, dude, dream clients.

I remember just talking with them and having a great time, everything was meshing. It was all coming together. I had closed that seriously painful listing mentioned before and was feeling ok for a minute. I started talking with them about what they were looking for and why they were moving here, and just shooting the shit about life in general. And then she asked, "Do you have a business card?" I said, "Yes." She goes, "I want it. We want to work with you." My jaw hit the floor. I was like, $750,000 budget and they want to work with me?! I was already calculating the math, like, okay, oh, my goodness. This is $18,000. Holy crap, I'm *finally* going to be rich.

At the time, after every open house, the one thing that I did was I would always turn on my cell camera, and I would shoot a video thanking the people that I had a connection with for visiting the house. So I did that with these two. "Hey, guys! Thank you so much for coming," I'd start out. Then I'd go over what we talked about in respect to their dream house, including their criteria and everything else. The clients ate this up. If you've heard anything in this entire book, it is that I always went with video, and it created this connection, and I never fully understood what I was doing. I just went all-in with the video.

I would send everybody the video right after they left. I did the same for them, and they loved it. So, Jesse and I went and started showing them $700,000 - $800,000 houses. I brought Jesse with me, stating, "Dude, you're coming. I'm not letting these people slip through the cracks." He agreed. And let me tell you, we did everything for these people. For me this was the biggest potential deal I'd ever had, so we worked with them flat-out for a couple of weeks. Problem was, they never could quite find the right house. Then all of a sudden, they kind of just went missing. I'd set them up on drip emails because they wanted to see houses at such and such price. Then all of a sudden, a reply comes in for one of my drip emails...

Hey, Jackson, we found our house. We do not need your services anymore. Good luck with your career.

Honestly, I was about to punch a hole through my computer. I was like, how? And I don't remember if I responded. I think I was probably so mad that I just let it go. And that's just kind of how I am. I don't deal with confrontation, but I remember that it irked me so bad. I thought, how the hell could they do that? And what agent out there stole you from me? That was really where my mind went. What agent stole you from me? I want to go kick the shit out of them now. I don't know to this day where they went. My guess is probably a new construction home, and the sales agent got them whatever it was. But that hurt.

So, back to the drawing board. Now I'm just hanging out in the brokerage office – it was my comfort place. There were a lot of other agents in this particular brokerage that didn't do any production, so there were a lot of meetings, sales meetings, technology meetings, and classes, and I just felt like at least I was doing the busy work. Man, that was a depressing time. I was starting to realize that I was never going to be able to chase clients, much less close them. At this point, I'm kind of like, man, I can go back to being lineman. That way, I could travel and make actual money. As I'm sure you've experienced more than once, there's that shit that just wears you down.

So, I was right on the verge of quitting. In my mind, I'm just like, 'I can't do this real estate thing, dude. I'm in a new market and depressed.' Basically, I was going into that office because there were other agents in there not producing. We could just bitch and moan together and pour more time into trying to learn about real estate than actually getting deals. I don't even know if I've ever told Jesse about it, but it was a low point, very low. I felt like a loser. I had two kids, and I made this huge leap of faith to get into real estate, and it wasn't working out. I had a goal of 25 deals and then later on 50 deals. I'm in month 8 of shooting hundreds of videos, with nothing sticking; of going to hundreds of open houses, cold calling clients and having the clients I did get just ditch me.

I looked at my kids like, and thought I was the biggest mess up. Thinking 'I got to move them back to Idaho, but I can't just move them again. I can't do this. My wife is just the best, and I'm not going to tell her how hard it was for me. I have to be positive.' and I'm a glass-half-full guy. It was just the time, and I had to do something. Since I hated cold calling and open houses so much, I thought, I didn't know what I was going to do. That particular fact must've been out there in the ol' universe because at that moment, Mr. J. Dau gives me a call. He says, "Hey, man, what's going on?" "Nothing, at this point," I respond cautiously. He's growing, he's closing homes, he's killing it. But all he wants is this marketing company. He wants to change the landscape of real estate. He wants a media company, not just a real estate office. And I was doing all of that for him, all the videos; shooting local videos and doing interviews. But nothing was sticking the way we wanted. I was just really trying to figure it all out. Watching all the other real estate agents around the area, copying their videos, and it didn't work.

Jesse must've sensed something was off because, one day, he just asked me flat out, "Hey, man, I know you got a wife and the kids, and you haven't made any money really yet. Are you okay?" I said, "Yeah, man, I'm good. Yeah, no problem." He's like, "No, dude, are you okay?" I told him then, "Not really. I mean, basically, any savings that I had are all gone now. The truth was out, so I continued, "Yeah, dude, I'm not doing too good. This shit is so hard. And I love doing the videos, but it's not paying." He goes, "Jackson, I'm getting to the point where I'm so busy right now. I just want to bring you on as a partner. I've been thinking about it. I need help just generally picking up signs, lock boxes, you know, marketing efforts, showing clients, whatever. I'll just give you 20% of my business, and look, you're putting in work that 99% of these realtors aren't, right? You're doing all this video stuff. Something's going to go one of these days. I don't know what it is, Jackson, but it's going to go. And the day that happens and your business equals mine, we will split everything 50-50 going forward." Like I said before, killer partner to have. He cares about people, and it shows.

When he said that, first of all, I wanted to cry and hug him. He saw something in me and knew we could join forces and knock this shit outta the park. I was shooting all these videos every day and doing all the social media marketing and all these funnels, and he was paying attention to all that.

Jesse giving me 20% of his business to go do lock boxes and signs, it was the greatest fucking job I've ever had in my life. I was like, 'give me more, give me more.' Send me across town. I don't give a shit where you send me. I don't care how many lock boxes you need. I don't care where you need it. I'll dig the signs for you. That's how much it meant to me to just be able to make enough money to actually come home with a paycheck for my kids, and my wife.

I get the mentality of why people get burned out and quit, and I got to thank my homie for bailing me out. The dude was bailing me out because I was *so freaking close* to quitting. Weirdly, it added a layer of extra pressure. That didn't hit for a couple of weeks, because he had some closings in the pipeline, and I started getting 20% of the commissions, and he did big homes, so I started getting paid. But now, I'm not bringing anything to the damn table. And in my mind, that meant bringing in closed deals, right? But Jesse knew I hated that shit, and he doesn't believe in doing stuff you hate doing for too long, if at all. He said what he meant, and what he meant was 'Jackson, I'm going to give you 20% of my business because I want you to continue doing what you're doing with the media stuff.'

So I went all-in on the video. Now I've got this added pressure because I'm not bringing any money in. I don't want to have to quit real estate. And this dude over here just gave me 20% of his business. Like, I better make this worth it.

And right at about this time, this is when we really went all-in on the *'Digital Mayor'* thing. What is it? Well, it's all about becoming someone who kinda owns their own real estate in the digital landscape. It's someone who creates content that people *want* to consume.

Like, they log-in to their Instagram, Facebook, Linked In, Twitter, or fire up YouTube on the daily, just to see what this person has to say. We had been listening to Gary Vaynerchuk, and he said, "If I got into real estate, I would crush everybody because I would be the digital mayor. Everybody would know me." Both Jesse and I really took to that.

So now that I had 20% of Jesse's business, I was going to build this media marketing team. I stepped away from the open houses (I now know that *pushing* to do something that you can't stand, won't get you anywhere). During the conversation I just mentioned, and a couple of subsequent ones, I told Jesse that I *hated* open houses and I could not stand cold calling. One of the coolest things about Jesse is, as long as you're honest with him up front, he's okay. He always wants to do things and try them, and if they don't work, he's the first to say, we're done, cut it off, let's move on. And that's, I think, a huge issue that people have. They'll try, especially in real estate, and they'll try ten different ways to get business, and they'll do each one of them just a little bit. That's what I did.

To go back and do it all again now, I'd immediately go all-in on video and not spend a day at open houses or cold calling. I wasted so much time and energy doing that, when I could have shot 10X more videos and figured it out quicker. But, as is life, that is not what happened. When we did go all-in, Jesse says, "Basically, if I'm paying you, it's time to go zero pity parties around here." And we did. We got *shit dooonnne.*

So we started doing shop, restaurant, and bar interviews. Seemed like the right approach. I mean, if you're moving to a new town, city or even another part of the same city, you want to know what it'll be like. As we've established, I couldn't doorknock or cold call to save my life when it came to slangin' houses, but when it came to door knocking on businesses to interview them, I hit them all.

As an aside: Jesse forced me to go door knocking once, and that was probably worse than any day of cold calling. As far as I'm concerned, door knocking is the shittiest thing to do on Planet Earth. I definitely didn't know any script for door knocking, so I called our mate (who was very good at knocking on doors and getting his foot in). He was the master of door-knocking. He got so many deals from door-knocking. It was crazy. So, before this day of absolute horror began, I called him. We went over his scripts, and he told me exactly what to say and do. So, I tried it and it definitely didn't work for me in the way that it works for him – not even close. It was brutal.

But I doorknocked for businesses, and it felt really good. It finally felt like I was in the place I was meant to be. I'm good with people, and that's one of the reasons I find it so hard to cold call. As hard as I try, it just feels like I'm bullshitting them. Not to say that others are, just to say that it's how I felt about it personally.

And you know what? These businesses loved us. We had business owners crying. We had them just tearing up. We'd also go to gyms, and we just went everywhere. Candy store? Yep. BBQ joint? Obviously. Basically, I'd pull over anyone at all and interview them. Here's a transcript from one of those interviews:

What's up, everybody? My name is Jackson Wilkey. I am with the NextHome Realty Connection. And today, we are at La Provence. Now, this is one of our favorite spots. And when anybody comes into town, we definitely take them here.

They got one of the best breakfasts you'll find in the entire Portland metro. They have their own bakery. They got great flights of Bloody Marys and mimosas. And the scenery you get outside the window, especially on a beautiful day like this, well. So let's go inside and check out what they got.

And I started putting those out there on Facebook. The crazy thing was I would go walking around with my family and kids, and people started going, "Dude, you're that video guy," and it felt amazing. I felt like any moment, it was all just gonna take off running. Jesse thought we were onto something, too. We were both getting notoriety, we were both being seen. It felt like, okay, this is it... This is how the Digital Mayor thing works. We had momentum. So I went harder and harder and shot better videos. We got drones. We hadn't actually gotten into GoPros yet, it was all on our phones. We hadn't done anything with YouTube yet. It was all Facebook, Instagram, and LinkedIn, and it was all short-form videos.

I would actually take the videos and edit them into perfect squares with the black bar up top, the black bar down the bottom, with the big white letters. So it stood out on Facebook ads, stood out on Facebook videos, and Instagram. I did it all every day, dozens of videos. And we got noticed.

And then one day, the boss mama of all boss mamas calls me. This dynamo of a woman is our top buyer's agent. Basically runs the whole Portland team. She said, "Hey, Jackson. I love your videos. Would you come to my son's elementary school and shoot a video for us?" I'm like, "Hell, yeah." She continues, "We do a big banquet every year, and it raises a ton of money for the school." I started to get to know her more than just at work. Her son has Dyslexia, so she's such a badass that she said, "Screw it. If they're not going to help my kid, I'm going to raise a bunch of money so that they have to." She took it upon herself to raise all of this money and do these massive conventions and all these auctions to bring all this money to the school. Her son got all the help he needed. She is the GOAT.

So, she wanted to do a video for this big gala that she was putting on, and I told her we'd definitely do it. So Jesse and I went there. We interviewed these kids, and made this badass video, Vlog style. Kids shootin' hoops, kids jump ropin', teachers interviewing them too. We're dancing with the kids, which is my favorite thing to do anyway because I'm the biggest kid ever and I got kids. It was just amazing. And she says, "I don't care what you sell, what you do, you just put it at the end of the video." So, at the end of the video, Jesse and I stood in front of the elementary school sign and said, "Hey, we did this for you guys. Tonight at this gala, make sure you're spending your money because it goes right to all of these kids and to your kids. And we want you to be a part of this." Then we told viewers that, as local real estate agents, 5% or 10% of every single deal we close over the next year, that money will be donated right to the school.

The woman who invited us there is the absolute GOAT at putting on these functions. She makes it so there are tons of prizes and so many cool things to do. They played our video, and everybody was cheering and telling us "great video."

That video blew up, and it got us to a lot of people. It wasn't what we were trying to do, we wanted to help in earnest. But it sent so many people our way. It honestly completely changed my trajectory from depression to hope, hope for the first time in a long time. I'm still not closing deals, but Jesse and I can just feel this thing is about to explode. The school thing was just huge. It was a big part of getting us started out. After that and a few other pieces, every video we were doing started opening up doors to more businesses and more people.

One day, I get this phone call: ring, ring "Hey, Jackson, this is [such and such], and I'm with the Beaverton Police Department."

I'm like, "what the hell did I do?!"

"No, man, what you've been doing in this community is amazing. All your videos show all these businesses. It's truly remarkable what you're doing in this community, and we want to do something with you too."

Here I am thinking, 'shit, the police department, let's goooo.' They said we're going to be contacting us in a week to start shooting videos.

"We want to highlight you and your business, and you do the same for us. We're going to talk about the community and safety protocols and that kind of stuff."

"Sign me up," I conclude.

I immediately called Jesse, "Guess who just called me?" Finally, after all of the guilt and coming so close to giving up tons of times, I *needed* to let him know that we were getting all these reach-outs from businesses. He's like, "Oh, shit. Dude, I'm telling you, this shit is about to blow up, dude. Hell, yeah."

The Beaverton Police Department never did reach out again, even though I tried to connect with them a couple more times. It just kind of fell through the cracks. Nonetheless, it was a huge win, and it let us know that we were going in the right direction–which was up.

Soon after, we got an incredible opportunity with another school. They have a program where every year, their fifth-grade class works with the Oregon Department of Fish and Wildlife to release a bunch of trout into Progress Lake. They wanted us to come and film this special event. So we're going to get some awesome footage of these kids releasing trout that they've been raising in their classrooms. If you didn't know, the stunning Progress Lake of Portland, Oregon, is stocked with trout every year so that you can go down there and fish. And the fifth graders at this elementary school play a big role in the fish you catch in that lake. It was awesome to be a part of.

I guess the moral of the story is to just do things that feel right, provide value for others when you're not expecting anything in return, and you'll be more than halfway there.

One thing about Jesse, and I'll talk about this more later, is that he's like the real estate version of Don King. He promotes better than any human I've ever met. But to be blatantly honest, there was a moment where it started to really piss me off. I felt like a lot of my work was being promoted and I wasn't getting as much recognition as I would've liked. But I forgot one key thing about Jesse: he just ain't that kinda person. He had my back, and in the whirlwind of all this recognition we *were* getting, I forgot that. It kinda taught me that, when you're arguing with anyone close to you, you gotta look at their intentions rather than the way you perceive them through your current lens. I didn't know his genius, right? He was into building a media company. And to do that, you got to be loud, and you got to be loud as hell.

Every single damn win we had, even while it wasn't closing sales, was bringing us closer to the big time.

He was blowing it all up on social media. We were becoming very well known in the local real estate scene. At this time, we're in these huge Facebook groups for real estate agents, and we're posting our success there. We're starting to get a lot of attention our way.

So in some regard, I felt like I was deserving of that 20% from Jesse. But at the core of my heart, being a hardcore blue-collar worker, I always felt like I had to work hourly for that. I still was feeling like I was taking this dude's money, but at least I was putting in all this effort. And that's the effort that he comments on a lot. I've heard him say time and again things like "I've just never seen a guy learn things so fast as Jackson does." But to me, it didn't seem like a lot. To me, I still had a timecard. Hours-in were the only thing that made the difference. It wasn't the reality, but it was how I was trained to be when I was a 9-5+ worker. When I was kept in my place; clocking in and out, day after day, and being told when to eat *and* when to shit.

We went on to do more school interviews, more shops, more restaurants, and more bars, and Jesse bailed me out financially. He'd made it clear from the beginning that we'd be doing this together and I'm glad I eventually started to remember that. The Bailout gave me the freedom to do all this stuff so that, together, we could take it to the next level.

Our next goal was to start teaching agents how to do what we did. Starting out, we watched a lot of Gary V. He would always tell people that they need to become a Digital Mayor. We decided to take his advice but we were going to do it better, bigger, and faster than anybody out there. Period.

And it's that kinda thinking that always brings out the best in the trolls and the naysayers, you know... when you're starting to make some real progress. So, at this point some other local real estate agents start throwing shade, *Oh, you're that annoying video guy. All you do is shoot videos.* The (much) classier agents had the opposite to say, *Yeah, what you're doing is badass. Man, I wish I could do that video stuff.*

Not only are we the digital mayors, and we're blowing that shit up, and all these agents are wondering how we're doing what we're doing–the clever ones wanted to learn it. Rather than kicking back and talking smack, they knew we were onto something that could seriously help them too.

So that was Jesse's next big venture. And that's how his mind works–there is never a stagnant moment in that guy's brain. He's always building another business, another revenue stream. Constantly. The dude pissed me off more times than you could imagine, but he was pushing me to my limits. He was an incredible coach with raw talent, and here I am being a crying ass like, *you're pushing me too hard.* All the while, he's getting me to win championships.

He says, "Jackson, we're going to build out a digital mayor group. We're going to teach agents how to do this." He always had that mindset that not only is this just real estate sales, but it's also way bigger than that. He had this vision forever of a media company, and that media company not only sold real estate but taught agents how to sell real estate. And at the core, all that might seem greedy and money hungry. He and I both love fucking helping people. There's nothing more passionate than that man helping people. That showed by giving me part of his business and bailing me out. He realized that if he pushed me in the right direction and continued to push past my whining, we'd be able to take this shit to the next level. So that's when *Digital Mayor Now* was born. Complete with podcast, and everything else. We were Digital Mayors Now.

CHAPTER 6

The Digital Mayor

"When you decide to become the
Digital Mayor of your town, everything
fundamentally changes"

– Gary Vaynerchuk

After the above quote, Gary V goes on to explain what he means by the term 'Digital Mayor.' He says that, in order to make great strides, you need to become a media company *as well as* a real estate agent. You need to own your local digital real estate before fully dominating the physical world around you. What does that mean? Providing value to the end user.

Rather than creating videos that serve you and (pretty much) only you, create videos that solve a problem for your audience. Just that one small shift will begin to build your reputation and make you an agent that people want to work with.

So, now that Jesse gave me 20% of his business and I was focused on the marketing side of things, we started to grow. We started really helping agents to walk the Digital Mayor path. And I know that we became known for being able to work YouTube for real estate, but we weren't even doing YouTube at the time. I did not invent this; I like to pay my dividends and give my respects to who I got the idea from. But then how I took that idea and made it into what it is today.

At this point, we're going all-in, Jesse's like, "Look, you need to go all in on this." The whole goal was to get me mentally freed up to where I could continue doing this video stuff and get our message and our brand out there; build a real estate team, and ultimately equate or surpass Jesse's current business (spoiler: we've done that now). Once that happened, we would go to a full 50/50 partnership.

Right about this time, we're having a lot of success with the videos in the eyes and opinions of other real estate agents. I was just kind of doing the videos because I loved it, and I knew it was a way that I wanted to get business. I had no idea how to do it, but Jesse's big vision was to have an epic media company that sells real estate. He always talked about the big picture. He was reading books on it, binge-watching Gary V vids, and walking the talk too.

To be brutally honest, I was just so damn broke and completely lost. I didn't care about any of that shit. I never thought that far ahead and that big either. I would ask him a lot of times, "Do you actually think it will make you a quarter million dollars from selling real estate or a million dollars?" He's like, "Fuck yeah." Like it was just so easy for him. He already knew it. He just needed to get into this business and he needed someone who loved doing the creative. That's where I came in.

So at this time, Jesse's like, "Okay, do you need an office?" I'm like, well, "I'm dead-ass broke. So it's up to you, man." He goes, "No, dude, do you want an office?" Yes, I wanted the office. I was working from my little 3-bedroom, 2-bathroom townhouse. I was using my third child's room, who was an infant at the time. It had a crib in there, and there was zero space. I know that a 3-bedroom, 2 bath townhouse doesn't sound that small, but this was in Portland, where tiny is always an option. To give you an idea; you'd walk through the garage door to get in and you would be greeted by a tiny-ass kitchen. The rest is (fortunately) history. Three little small kids in the house, and it was brutal. But I had to do what I had to do, and so Jesse brought that up, and in my mind, I'm seeing all these marketing companies with super cool offices. In my mind, I was thinking "get me that shit and we'll make a million dollars."

So, I agreed. Besides, I would need to do podcasts soon enough and couldn't do that from home." So, boom, he rents this thing out. I end up putting all the wood flooring in there and we make the place look pretty damn cool, if I might say so. We were even going to pay these graffiti artists to come in and tag the walls up (but ended up just getting right to work). We had a BIG vision.

Back when I was doing the Facebook advertising stuff, I learned it via a reputable coaching program, it was like $500 and a month to learn it. So I learned it fast. I started to form a friendship with the two dudes who were teaching most of the classes. These guys are super sharp and just totally chill. They basically ran this company for a famous Facebook ads coach. We get talking and these guys commend us on our new Digital Mayor thing we had going. As we got deeper into the conversation, we all realized that the 4 of us together could be unstoppable.

We're about to launch Digital Mayor Now with a Facebook group, podcast, and a proper website. Our goal was to help agents with their video marketing. So, all four of us got on camera and introduced ourselves and what we were doing.

The two other dudes had had a lot of success in helping marketing companies to build Facebook groups. These groups were charging $49-199 a month to join and then you continuously teach the audience in that group. Our business plan for Digital Mayor Now was to set one of these things up and get a bunch of these agents in there. I'm being honest with you. That was it.

In the real estate world, Jesse and I had eyeballs on us. A lot of people were watching what we were building. We were loud, and we were everywhere. I always say that Jesse is the Don King of real estate. He was always pimping our videos out there everywhere to everybody. So, we were going to show others how to do videos and how to sell.

The new guys had made this business plan for us, and it was going to cost something. At the exact same time, I was dead broke, again. Yes, Jesse gave me 20% of his business, but I didn't have a whole helluva lot padding out my bank account. So the dudes say, "Guys, you're doing all these videos about the Digital Mayor stuff, and it's badass, but you got to do more with it. You guys have got to create these Facebook groups." At that time, Jesse's longtime sales coach was also getting in on this Facebook groups action. He had a massive 40,000 agents who had joined to hear what he had to say. He echoed what had been previously said and advised that we build out a group too. As this played out, we started to realize that this approach could be an absolute gold mine. Particularly with all the content and value we were providing–no other agents are doing this in a Facebook group.

The package they built out for us was around $5,000, if I'm not mistaken. That initial amount was to set it up and then there would be $2,800 a month for managing the group, running some small ads, website setup and writing 3 blog posts a week. They would also take our videos and get them edited and uploaded to YouTube. In my mind, I'm thinking this is going to be the most badass thing on planet Earth.

One problem: I didn't quite have the money and I didn't want to go to my parents about it. My dad's one of those guys who made $30-40k a year and pinched pennies and never had a vehicle payment. So he had the money, but I don't know; I just didn't want to ask him. And then there was Jerde, my buddy who I talked about in one of the chapters before. One crazy asshole. I knew he had a shitload of money, and I knew he was my best friend. So I called up Garett, "Garett, man. Hey dude, I've got literally like 15 grand in my savings account, period. I'm not making any money. I got to get this business up and going. I don't want to just completely devour my savings, my everything, right? That's like I've been living off savings." Before even getting any more words, he goes, "How much do you need when you need it?" Even though he hadn't asked for further explanation, I continued, "Bro, I'm telling you right now, I'll pay you back. I ain't one of our shitty friends who's just gonna ghost you, and this is just to get my business going. I don't even know if I'm going to spend any of this money, but I do not want to get into my savings because that's going to just tear my wife and me up. And I just don't want that pressure, man. So I'll pay you back. I just need the money." He's like, "Bro, just send me the wiring instructions. I'll wire it to you today." I said, "I love you, dude, I love you."

So what did I do? Send them the wrong wiring instructions. I freaked out, I put the wrong number in there, and he sent it, and I didn't get it. I went back and looked at the number I gave, it was the wrong number. Could've been bad, but thankfully it didn't go to anyone else's account. That took like five days to correct. He ended up sending me that 20 grand. You know it's like when you get a pile of cash you've been waiting on? Maybe a commission check, for example? The minute that money comes in, you know everything will be smooth sailing. Maybe you'll invest it and just make hand-over-fist returns on it. Whatever you're going to do, it's going to be good. We start this thing up. I pay the five grand plus another twenty eight hundred to get going. Yet, two months into this thing, and I literally have 2-3 grand left of that 20. It was a definite "oh, fuck" moment.

We had everything set up under our "Now" branding. There was Beavertonnow.com, PearlDistrictnow.com and RealAgentnow.com. One of our groups was under the Beaverton Now. If you go to Facebook today, you can still see all of the OG videos we have up on that group. And you know what? The only people that ever liked and shared and looked at it were Jesse, my mom, my dad, my mother-in-law, my brother-in-law, and one of our real estate friends. That was it.

After a couple of months, I had to pay attention to the fact that it just wasn't working. And then the blogs weren't really getting to us. These dudes are sharp and we had a great time with them, but it was just way too much for two dudes to handle. It fell, and it fell fast. After two months, I called them up, "I can't afford to pay you guys another three grand this month. I have to save this money. So let's just put me on a hold, dude." They understood, responding with "I get it bro. It's all good. Just do what you got to do for your family."

After that, I continue doing the videos and posting them to our Beaverton Now group, and it's just not working. If you've ever started a Facebook group, where you post like three or four times a day, you may have noticed an initial surge that dies down after a few weeks. It sucks.

Now during this process with our group, the whole Digital Mayor thing actually started to take off. So we created a free group and a podcast too. Before we started to record the podcast, Jesse and I got into this room at our office, and we got those giant-ass pieces of paper that stick on the wall. We filled out 12 of these things. We wanted to map out the whole plan this time. It went something like this: 1) Creating Facebook groups, 2) Facebook ads, 3) blogging, and continued all the way through the 12th, which was YouTube. Kinda tricky because we had no idea how to use YouTube at the time.

We'd decided that as Digital Mayors, we had to be everywhere. We had to be front and center of every single social media platform, period. If you've followed me for any length, you know that's one of our biggest mistakes of all time. We didn't know that, and nobody else knew either because not one person was teaching the right shit.

So I'm doing these podcasts, and talking to all these different real estate agents. This is when I started to wonder *did any of these videos really work for Real Estate*? I'm interviewing agents from everywhere. What I would do is go to these real estate Facebook video groups, and find agents that were always posting in there and posting their videos, and I would ask them to join me on the podcast. There are groups like that where you just share your videos with a bunch of Realtors. It's ridiculous. I did it a lot, and so I would interview others who did too. Most of them were all about their videos and how many views they got on them. At the end of each talk, I'd ask them "how much business are you getting from your videos?" It was a tough question for people to answer, many citing that it wasn't something that was easily quantifiable. That's because it wasn't getting them business, just views and likes.

When I realized that no-one was getting business from these videos, I started to get a little bit disgruntled. I was using Jesse's money, I had this $20,000 loan from Jerde, and I'm busting my ass teaching all these agents how to do this. I wasn't feeling at all motivated by any of it, and there's only so long you can keep that up.

One of my next interviews on the podcast was with a very well-known Hollywood editor turned real estate agent. This guy made the sickest videos. He had a *Dominate with Video* course that he was slanging. It was just a video editing course, but when you get going and video, editing is key. When you see somebody's killer video, you want to know how they did it. He edited for 18 years in Hollywood, so his videos were like nothing I'd ever seen before, and they were so cool. We got chatting after his interview, and he asked me if I'd heard of this woman who was killing it on YouTube as an agent. So, I reached out to this woman and managed to get her on the podcast. One thing she mentioned that really stood out for me was a 'Pros and Cons' video that she'd done. This thing had really taken off. She also talked about how YouTube wasn't her favorite at first. She was actually a blog writer. She relocated a ton because of her husband's military. It's really the main podcast that I remember out of all of them because it's just so different. At one point she says, "I'm relocating to all these different areas and I don't know anybody, so I just write blogs and get leads from them. I found out that, after Google bought YouTube, you could include YouTube videos in blogs and it would help you rank better." She continues, "I was just finding random videos and putting them in my blogs, and then I realized, well, shit, I might as well make my own videos." So she started doing that and that was kind of her start on YouTube. At the end of the interview, I asked her my go-to closing questions, "how much business do you get from your videos?" Surprisingly, she came back with "Oh, actually I have a closing today from one, and we've closed, you know, 6 deals." Now in shock, I reply, "You shitting me? Like you *actually* close deals?" Nodding, she responds, "Yeah, I got one today. I have one next month." That was the first time I'd ever heard about somebody getting actual business from video. This is also the point of my life when I am doing more videos than any human could possibly handle. Every podcast interview I did had me learning new techniques that those agents were using.

Right after that, another guy, who I worked with at the title company before, calls me "I see all the videos you're doing. I just want to let you know that I did that at one point. I just want to talk to you about some stuff." I say, "Okay."

He came into our office and Jesse and I sat down with him. He started by saying "I see all those Digital Mayor videos you guys are doing and I just want to let you know that we did a lot of that too." Before he got to the title company, he had been working for this brokerage and they created all these Digital Mayor videos. But this guy's actual specialty was SEO. He knows SEO like crazy. He built a bunch of websites with all these blogs and backlink them and was just driving in massive traffic, and leads. So he was getting a ton of leads from the websites and then they went all-in on the Digital Mayor stuff. They were cranking out videos about shops, restaurants, and bars. Reflecting upon it, he said "Dude, we never got a phone call. It doesn't work. That's when we knew we had to go back to just blog writing." To this day, I've actually heard from people that he's the one who made my YouTube career kickoff but it wasn't. He didn't talk about YouTube. He talked about blog writing. But he definitely helped us correct our path and validated what I had been pondering on. With that, I started writing some blogs and sending them to him for a quick checkover. They were atrocious, by the way. I started shooting the videos and putting them in there. So what I got from him was a start in understanding SEO and it's very important place in the content marketing ecosystem. You need to be where people are searching for answers–being on Facebook and Instagram just didn't work. People don't give two shits about that stuff when buying and selling homes. So, it was kind of a tough pill to swallow, but it was also reaffirming.

Jesse didn't trust what the guy was saying, so it was in one ear out the other, but it hit me a little bit harder because I was the one putting in the video hours. I'd been working through the night, up before the kids, editing and shooting videos.

Now, this is when I start kind of going to the Facebook group for the woman I had interviewed before because it was a super valuable talk we had and I knew she was onto something. The group was predicated on likes, comments, and shares. So her big thing was to tell people to shoot YouTube videos and drop them in the group so that everyone could comment, like, subscribe and help each other out. I also noticed that she was teaching all these inspection, escrow, property tours, short videos, and such. So I started doing that because she was closing deals off of them, so I could too, right? I'm like shit, if she's closing deals, I will. And I'll never forget looking and thinking 'why the hell is she shooting these videos? They don't get any views!' But she was still closing deals, and her *Pros and Cons* video had over 20,000 views. So it worked for her. I tried shooting the same style of videos. The problem was that I had to script everything. The themes were on escrow inspection, market updates, etc. I don't know anything about real estate. I honestly didn't give two shits about real estate. So, if I was bored with the subject matter, why would anybody else watch them? However, when you're told something over and over, sometimes you just continue to do it. I think all of us have probably been there, when you have to do something, you just don't really like doing, you force it, it feels like forever, and it's really tough. That's kind of what YouTube was for me in the beginning.

I had about 125 videos before I started, they're all unlisted now because they murdered my channel. Then I decided to do my own *Pros and Cons* video. To this day, it has 50-60 thousand views. It drives a lot of traffic. Right after posting, I got like six views on this video and I'm like, 'why am I only getting six views?' I didn't understand why hers had 20,000 and that led me to the conclusion that YouTube sucked. So I quit for a month or two. Then I did another video on cost of living, and I filled it with market updates, property tours, listing videos or whatever she was recommending, and I would put them all on our Facebook group as well. The YouTube channel did nothing. We weren't ranking for anything, and I kind of gave up. I was still going all-in on the 'day in the life of the real estate agent' vlogs, doing our community stuff, trying to keep the Facebook group alive. YouTube was just in the back of my mind, but it wasn't working for me. I didn't know anything about thumbnails, analytics, or click-through rates. None of that was being taught. But after being in there for a while, I started to notice that learning about all that might just be the play. So I got obsessed.

Finally, I realized that I didn't like the videos I was seeing on YouTube. So, I began to play around with the YouTube search filters. Filtering out market updates and such, just for Portland, I saw that there were at least 20 different realtors doing those. And each one of these videos had three views, seven views, nine views, one view, a hundred views... But what if I just typed in 'Portland, Oregon'? When I did, the top 10 videos that came up had titles such as '10 Worst Areas to Live in Portland, Oregon', 'Pros and Cons of Living in Portland, Oregon', 'AVOID Moving to Portland, Oregon'. Funny thing was, none of the people posting them were real estate agents. It was all these National brand YouTubers, mostly people who hid behind the camera–you'll never see their faces. And honestly, they probably read somebody else's blog, and rattle off 10 key points. They shot these for every major city across the country, and they were getting 100,000 views, 2.5 million views. That's when we changed course again and started to shoot content about moving to the city and its suburbs. After all, why would I focus on the other real estate videos I had been shooting if they didn't work?

I myself had just moved to Portland, Oregon, a year and a half before. My wife and I had all these things driving us crazy. We had no clue as to where to live. I'd show our friend Zach, "Oh dude, check out this house. What about this area?" He often comes back with, "NO. Do not move to that area. It's bad, bad." It was so frustrating not to know the area. But it all started clicking–YouTube wasn't a pile of shit after all, I just hadn't been looking at it from the right angle yet. It's a major hub where people go to seek out information, real information. Information that would actually help them make one of the most major life decisions a person could make. Where you chose to live can change your trajectory entirely.

To make this YouTube thing work, I had to figure out how to properly research keywords, words that real people were using in their online searches. I started out using KeyWords Everywhere. It was super interesting at first, but I found out that it was pulling its information from Google and not YouTube specifically. It was not really giving me the correct information because people search differently when they're looking for written content vs YouTube content. Not only that, but keyword competition can be completely different from one platform to the next.

To this day I still have a document on my computer called *YouTube Fucking Goldmine.* This compilation of killer finds began when I started doing keyword research into phrases that were not real estate related. I figured that, in order to get a leg up on the local competition, it had to be about Portland, Oregon. After that, I started discovering that there were lots of cities and suburbs that were being searched 4,000-10,000 times a month. Not only that, but people were searching for cities and suburbs many more times a month on YouTube as opposed to Google. Hell. Yeah.

On the *YouTube Fucking Goldmine* doc, I have all of these cities, sectors, top neighborhoods with their search number next to them. I realized that this was what I needed to be shooting. Much like McDonald's actually made their fortune in the real estate that their restaurants are on, I knew that we had to own the keywords for these cities and suburbs, not for the real estate market. It all started hitting me at once–this is what people want. They want to search the city, and they want to find videos about it, just like we did when moving to Portland. On that note, I remember searching 'Beaverton' and the result at the time was one video, shot vertically on a cell phone, of somebody at a Beaverton Farmers Market. That was the information that people had.

At the time, one of the top city-style videos on YouTube was *Best Areas to Live in Portland*, and it wasn't even from a real estate agent. That was it, I told Jesse we're going to go shoot a video featuring the top five neighborhoods in Portland. I didn't know how we're going to do it, but we're going to go through the entire Portland metro and make it happen.

Meanwhile, I became obsessed with YouTube. I'd decided to tune out every real estate agent and digital marketer out there. Gary V, all of them. I'm done with you guys. I'm going to learn from YouTubers how to do this shit and I'm going to do it right. That one lightbulb moment is what paved the way for what we've done and how we've helped these thousands of agents to do the same. It's been a crazy ride, but the Digital Mayor Now is dead, and the real estate vlog is alive.

In the new vlog, we featured what it's like to work, eat, sleep, live, and play in cities on a local level. And we had no idea what we were doing. We started with a phone then went to GoPro. Had no idea about metadata, tagging, descriptions and custom thumbnails. None of that. It was a wild ride, but we made it.

CHAPTER 7

Becoming a YouTuber

So now I decided I'm going all-in with this YouTube thing, but I got to figure it out. I got to get obsessed with it, spending countless days, hours, nights, weekends, and months studying the inner workings of YouTube. I was still doing traditional real estate, as Jesse had given me part of his business. Not too much cold calling but I still was holding open houses. What that meant was watching YouTube and, once again, hoping nobody showed up.

During the day, I would listen to YouTube videos while I drove, and would watch them all night as well. It's just all I did. So what I had to do is just kind of get rid of all the noise. The noise in the real estate industry, the Facebook groups, gurus and anyone else talking about real estate marketing tactics. Why? Most of them were just full of shit. It was really just a case of getting down to the nitty-gritty of YouTube.

The first useful content creator I found on YouTube, Nick Nimmin, had a very entertaining vibe about him.

He was all about helping people grow their YouTube channels. He'd slam his face up to the camera with his big ol' bald head. Nick's videos had a ton of jump cuts and killer thumbnails. His videos were along the lines of 'How to get your first 1,000 subscribers, and 'how to grow a YouTube channel as a beginner.' He'd been doing it for a long time, and his stuff was actually pretty killer. He was also kind of annoying. But at the same time, he was getting views and I liked his style. He was really big on getting your thumbnails right, optimizing intros, placing hooks, and relaying what your channel is about. So the big takeaway I got from him was how to start out videos by hooking people.

In the real estate industry, what is always taught is: "Hi, my name is Jackson Wilkey. I'm a local real estate agent." That's where we lose people. Whenever I would watch this guy's videos, he'd hook me at the very beginning, "Hey, you're starting a channel, and your videos aren't ranking. In this video, I'm going to teach you five ways to rank your video better." In my mind, I'm doing these pros and cons videos, and my shit ain't ranking. A video like that would answer my question in full. Then he would do another one, "Hey, are you new to YouTube, and you want to grow and get more subscribers? In this video, I'm going to teach you how to get more subscribers." He knew that people want to click on a video and quickly know if it was going to help them answer a burning question. If a video can't do that, most people will click away to find one that does have that promise laid out in the first few seconds.

After a while of doing all this and watching people like this Brian G. Johnson, I started to understand that YouTube is a search engine. To rank, we absolutely had to have eye-catching titles, well-researched keywords, and we needed to hook people right in the beginning. But what about a script? Did you need one? I did create a video script structure that thousands of agents are still using today. Hell, some agents even try to teach it as if it's theirs. Personally, I no longer script because it can come off as kinda plastic. But I created and shared it because one of the biggest mistakes that new agent YouTubers make is talking about themselves instead of answering a question. After analyzing all these YouTube posts, I realized that I had hundreds of videos talking about myself or my open house, or my listing. They were all "me, me & me.' I call them 'me, me, my' videos. And that just isn't how it works.

One day, we shoot this video. This one's painful to recall because this was the first video that I hired a videographer and an editor for. I'm dressed up to the nines, polished like a shiny penny, and I sound like a damn news anchor. It's perfect. It took us 6 hours to shoot this two-minute video, and was fully scripted. It started with my name and went on to explain how I was a top local expert. When in actual fact, I was brand new to the market and didn't know goddamn thing. But this one took me two weeks to get back, and it cost me over $1,200. And you know what? I didn't get shit from it. Here's how that video started "My name is Jackson Wilkey. I'm with NextHome Realty Connection and I get to show you this wonderful place I call home."

Ouch. But that's what most real estate agents do: "Hi, I'm the top local agent here. I'm the greatest ever. And if you're thinking of buying or selling, call me." With that we didn't answer the consumer's questions. YouTube is a search engine. It's content marketing. The number one thing about content marketing is answering the consumers' questions (read that again).

Another huge element of successful YouTube channels is having a niche. When I started in real estate, we were being taught to just showcase everything. Our YouTube channel had a little bit about our city and our listings. But it also had; how to help real estate agents grow their business, social media marketing, etc. We were supposed to just kind of put every single aspect of our life, our business, our city on one channel. But if you shoot a bunch of videos about Portland, Oregon, and then all of a sudden, you hit your audience with these videos about creating Facebook ads for real estate and how to do real estate marketing, they're going to be immediately turned off by that. They're not going to watch that style of video. With that your click-through rates and your average view rate are going to plummet. This is what I started understanding; the channel truly needed to be about its niche. At that time, I was trying to shoot videos about Portland, but yet my channel was all about me and sales and real estate–my number and my email. It was just completely all about Jackson Wilkey and real estate. Not one thing that anybody was searching for.

Back when viewing Nick's channel, I noticed that his about section was all about the niche of helping people grow their YouTube channels. His about section said something that equated to: 'Hi, my name is Nick. I grow YouTube channels, and I'm going to teach you today's methods for getting your first thousand subscribers to your channel.' Simple and to the point, but most importantly, it's useful. So, his whole channel, the about section and all descriptions were about growing YouTube channels.

Then I found a YouTube video marketing strategist, Brian G.Johnson. This dude had the best videos about understanding the analytics side of things. He did these deep dives into average view durations, traffic sources, click-through rates, analytics, metadata, and competition. I was like, this is the shit right here. He would break down the analytics with a ton of graphs and charts, and would point arrows at everything. In that, this guy taught me that average view durations were the most important part of ranking videos. Also metadata, building out your description correctly, using a YouTube-specific analytics program, and thumbnails are super important. He'd show examples of all these YouTubers who, even if they had a million subscribers, he could eventually outrank them because they hadn't filled out descriptions or tags correctly nor leveraged the best keywords. Many, he remarked, could use better thumbnails, too.

Bold statement, but after everything I learned and practiced, I do not believe there's a person on this earth who could go toe-to-toe with me when it comes to analytics. I can look at your analytics and your traffic sources, and tell you exactly how to get longer average view durations and how to grow your channel. I can tell you that if your YouTube traffic source has 80% of your traffic, meaning that 80% of the people finding your YouTube channel are coming from YouTube search, your videos are just way too short. At the time of writing this, 1-3 minute videos are way too short. If 45%-50% of your traffic is coming from YouTube searches, your videos are probably closer to 4-6 minutes long.

Another point that this other dude really hammered home was that, not only do you have to have good average view durations, but you've got to have incredible b-roll. He goes on to say, "do you notice in my videos I'm constantly changing the scene to all these graphs, to having these arrows? Literally, by putting words and titles on your video, it captures people's attention, and keeps them there." He iterated several times that simple sound effects can also increase average view durations.

Another trend I noticed with these dudes was that they'd take their top video titles and keep reshooting them every month, just a little different each time. When you start doing YouTube, you're going to feel like you're doing repetitive content, and it can really mess with you mentally. You're probably going to think that you have to find new, fresh ideas all the time. It's actually the opposite. You need to figure out your traffic sources, understand what people are searching for and finding to get to your channel, and just hammer the shit out of those keywords over and over again to get it in front of new eyeballs.

You need to understand your traffic source, keywords, channel keywords, and the top drivers of your channel, and then start making better, longer videos. I'm sure you've heard the saying 'hey, people only have an attention span of 6 seconds, it's less than a goldfish.' Nope, not on YouTube where people go to *learn* things. Some of the highest ranking videos are around 30 minutes long! If you hook people, keep them interested with killer graphics and sound effects, promise that you'll answer their question, and ask them to stick around to the end to get the full answer, you'll get more eyes for longer. And that will push your video up in the YouTube algorithm.

When I stand on stage or I do my YouTube Lives, people have a lot of questions. My typical response is that everything always comes back to analytics, data, average view duration, and click-through rates. That's really what I'm always judging, traffic sources. It all came from Brian G. Johnson. He would say things like 'you're going to think you're making the greatest content of all time, and your analytics are going to slap you in the mouth.'

So, I'm already shooting these Vlogs about topics such *Top 5 Neighborhoods in Portland, Oregon*, and the like. With the help of Nick Nimmin on getting my calls to action in there and getting my intros and hooks, and then also Brian G. in understanding my traffic, I'm starting to rank videos, and the channel is starting to grow like crazy.

I went into my traffic sources, and the number one driver to my channel was YouTube search. And it always will be on the Portland channel because I put it behind the eight-ball for so long. Meaning that I was sharing my videos on social media to everyone, everywhere, and I wasn't getting organic data. This led to loads of issues that I have and will touch on further in this book. So anyways, when I clicked in to see *what* people were searching for to find us, I found out that the top driver to our Portland, Oregon, channel was *Vancouver, Washington.* I was like, "ho-ly shit!" I called up Jesse.

"Dude, you're licensed in Washington, right?"

Jesse: "Yeah."

Me: "How much do you know about Vancouver?"

Jesse: "Enough."

Me: "We need to start shooting videos up in Vancouver."

Jesse: "Why?"

Me: "It's the number one driver to our channel. I just learned

that. We have this backend area where you can look up your

traffic sources and see how people are searching and finding

our channel. The number one thing is Vancouver, Washington.

We can dominate that market too."

So we drove up the next day and shot a *Living in Vancouver, Washington* video as well as a *Vancouver vs Portland*. Without learning about analytics, I would never have known to do videos for Vancouver, and I think last year, we probably did 20-plus million dollars in Vancouver. We also just hired a new Vancouver agent. Analytics don't lie.

When I started talking about analytics, everyone started hitting me up: "Jackson, I'm doing what you're saying, and nothing's working. Check out my channel." I'd go to look at their channel, and there'd be, like, 2-3 videos on it. One was about knitting sweaters, and another one was about the pros and cons of Florida. Then the third video would be about changing out the mud flaps on a '69 Bronco. Like, you're giving me nothing. You got to have a good 20 videos. Do two new videos a week, and you'll be ready in ten weeks. Then I can dive into your analytics, and your traffic sources, and I can tell you *exactly* what you need to do. We'll find out if your videos are too short, if you're not keeping people's attention, that your average view duration sucks. Then we'll find the top four keywords that you need to hammer, hammer, hammer on. With that, you will grow your channel, guaranteed.

That's really what I learned from Brian G. Johnson, it was more of the analytics side behind things. And Nick Nimmin is where I learned that the channel was not about me. Other valuable lessons were that you have to structure your videos correctly, you've got to hook these people and you need a call to action that is valuable. One of Nick Nimmin's big things was that you've got to get subscribers because subscribers, at the end of the day, tell YouTube that people like your content. That then translates into YouTube finding more people that like your style of videos. But you can't just tell people, "hey, subscribe to my channel." That's what most real estate agents do: 'Hi, thinking about buying or selling? Call me and make sure that you share this video with everybody.' No value given. We'll dig into more about the right style of CTA in the next chapter.

At this point in time, we're still in a Facebook community group for real estate agents. Every video we took, we shared it with the group because that's what was being taught. Unfortunately, even YouTube says that you should spread your videos far and wide across the social media platforms of the World Wide Web. But now I understand that youtube is a business. And, honestly, they don't give a shit what happens to your video. They just want people on their platform to feed ads. With that, I started noticing that if you want your videos to get recommended by YouTube, you need to have a strong organic search game.

At this point, we're creating some pretty awesome vlogs. Every day, we were out shooting videos. I'm shooting vids on the ground and Jesse was flying the drone. We had, like, 15 of these little micro SD chips. We're getting the footage loaded up, edited, and published. The channel is growing, now that I understand metadata and how to build out video descriptions properly. I learned how to make these custom descriptions so that we could rank. We even started leapfrogging other people's vids that had 500,000+ views, because they weren't even building out their description at all. They were just putting their websites in there and calling it a day. Then we'd share it with real estate Facebook group that we were a part of... and it's gone. Where the hell did it go?

I started noticing that posting on social media made it so that it stopped showing up on YouTube. I'm like, what the hell is going on? It was so damn frustrating. Average view durations, and click-through rates were plummeting. I called Jesse. There's a lot of me just calling Jesse up, and we talk all the time, especially when I learn a new thing on YouTube or when shit just hit the fan. So I call him, "Bro, we need to stop sharing these videos on social media." A bit shocked, because he had been sharing these things like crazy, Jesse comes back, "What do you mean?" I continue, "It's killing our channel. I can see it in the analytics. Every time we post a new video and upload it to YouTube, it ranks. It gets decent average view durations, click-through rates, and then, as soon as we start pumping it out there to everybody's Facebook groups, to our Facebook pages, to Instagram and all the things, it plummets. It pulls it out of ranking and messes with our data analytics. Everything is getting skewed." Jesse, still thinking I've lost the plot, says "Dude, no way. We have to keep posting. Even YouTube says to promote." Persistent, I say "Dude, I'm telling you right now, the data don't lie. Let's stop sharing it and see what happens." We did. Boom–that shit blew up.

Now I have gone against the opinions of some of the biggest YouTubers, not just real estate, but the biggest YouTubers in the world, and said this. In fact, I spoke at VIDFEST two different times. On the first occasion, I announced " I learned early on that sharing to other social media channels actually kills your YouTube channel. I can see it in the analytics. When I stopped doing it, I was getting a lot more organic search views, and YouTube was starting to recommend my videos, and my average view durations increased. Not only that, but the videos started ranking so much faster." People responded, 'I don't know about that.' and 'No dude, you're wrong.'

When I attended VIDFEST the second time, I was introduced as "The guy who said 'stop sharing on social media.'" Some of these massive YouTubers told me that, after I said what I said in the first VIDFEST, they experimented with not sharing to social, and their channels erupted.

If you understand YouTube, their number one goal is to get people to the platform to feed them advertisements. So, whichever videos keep people's attention the longest, that's typically whose video they're going to recommend. Those videos will hold the top spot for the specific keywords they rank for as well as, in many cases, similar keywords. The longer and more engaging the video, the more advertisements YouTube can squeeze in. When we were placing our videos in front of no-one but real estate agents, our friends, our mom and our dog sitter–well, those people don't give a shit about it. It has nothing to do with them. They're going to click on it just to help you. But when they click off, that is an average view duration of just a few seconds. When you paste it in front of hundreds of thousands of people, and they don't click on it, that's a terrible click-through rate. When you put it in a real estate Facebook group, and now all of your views are coming from realtors, the algorithm is trying to find more people like that to recommend your videos to. Problem is, they don't care either. That's when it hit me. It was *crushing* our channel. I don't care who says it, sharing to social jacks up your ranking.

I've traveled the country, started channels in eleven different markets, and when I found the agents to work with, the first thing I told them was, "Hey, we're going to shoot all these videos. They're going to be incredible. They're going to be badass. You're going to want to share them. Trust me, I know. Do not. If you share one of these videos on any one of your social media platforms, the partnership is over, and I will find somebody else to do it with." "All right, Jackson. I won't." They want to share so badly because they want to look cool, but it absolutely destroys your channel.

So one of the biggest things that I learned was understanding your data, your analytics, traffic sources, average view durations, and click-through rates. It's so important. I went down the craziest rabbit hole of split-testing thousands of thumbnails, and different titles; split-testing just one word in a title or one word in a thumbnail, and getting 1%-2%-3% better click-through rates at a time. I really went down this long path, but I learned a lot from those two guys.

Now that I understood the average view durations and allowing YouTube to place my videos, instead of me putting them on social media, we started getting better and better and better at these videos. I ain't going to lie, these vlogs were sick.

We sat down one day with our lender, who's still our team lender, Addy Nett. He was working at this bank, and his manager, or the owner of the bank, was a cool-ass dude. Addy was doing tons of video, we were doing video, and the owner was doing video. So, we sat down with the owner one day. He said, "You guys are making awesome videos. I've just never seen anybody out in the community shooting 15-20 minutes vlogs with all the drones and all of that information. It's one of the coolest things I've ever seen." He was big into the video stuff and, as a big bank owner, very much into the marketing techniques. "I've just never seen anything that cool. It's amazing," he says. "How much business are you getting from it?" And... it was like a bad memory because I had to say, "Nothing." We had been on this trajectory of shooting tons of content. We were growing like crazy. And honestly, we were big shit. Everybody was looking at our stuff, and I had to freaking sit there and tell this guy "nothing." I hadn't closed a damn deal from any of it. That's when an incredibly pivotal section of our journey comes in. The bank owner turns to me and very kindly says, "Jackson, have you ever told anybody to call you in your videos?" I tell him, "No, you can't. We've been taught that if you tell people to call you at the beginning, it's salesy, and they'll jump off your videos right away. Everybody knows if you say that, you're going to just be a salesy person, and no-one is going to call you. So you have to put it at the end of your video." Laughing, he continues, "Jackson, you have to tell people what to do in life. They're idiots, you have to tell them. You have to figure out how to incorporate a call to action at the *beginning* of your video. You have to tell people to call you."

Now, this is a bank owner, a dude who's crushed sales, a guy who's gotten a lot of business, so he knows how to ask for the business. If you read the whole beginning of this book, what's my biggest weakness? Asking for the business. Cold calling, door knocking, open houses. I'm shitty at it. I'd easily get up and talk in the middle of a party with a million people, but when it came to asking for the business, I was brutal at it. So I left that meeting knowing that the channel was growing, the videos were awesome, I got the hook down. I needed to take this guy's sage advice and find a way to get a valuable call to action in the beginning of these vids. To this day there are still people who have never closed deals from their YouTube channels, and they need to know how. I *needed* to know how.

One day, Jesse and I were going to shoot another Vlog. It was called 'Where to Live in Portland, Oregon, When Moving to Portland, Oregon.' We were going to go to the middle of downtown Portland and shoot on the Tilikum Crossing Bridge. The plan was to interview Jesse about the four different sections of Portland, and who lives there and who doesn't. Before Jesse showed up, he was a little bit late that day, I went to work getting this call to action in there. It had to be in the beginning, I had to tell people to subscribe and it had to be valuable. And it couldn't be salesy.

To get how it played out, I've transcribed that part of the actual video. It's a little bit longer, but I was trying to figure out that call to action. Take one:

Okay, so you've been thinking about moving over here to the Portland Metro, but you're just not quite sure about the perfect area for you, your family, or whoever's coming with you. Maybe you're bringing some pets with you. We're going to go over all the different areas of the Portland Metro because it is so diverse around here. So if you want to know the best place for you to live in the Portland Metro, stay tuned.

Take two:

Hi, my name is Jackson Wilkins with the Real Agents Now Group and Next Home Realty Connection right here in the Portland, Oregon, metro area. So today, we are going to do a video all about the different types of living all around the Portland Metro that's going to fit your lifestyle. So make sure you hit that subscribe button and click the little bell. We do so many videos about what it's like to live here that will answer a ton of your questions. Comment down below if there's an area you've been researching and you want to know more about; comment below. We'll go do a video on that or I'll go shoot a live video for you personally. So anyway, let's get to all the different styles of living you'll find in the Portland Metro.

The final take for our general intro:

All right. It is a beautiful day here. I'm on the Tilikum Crossing, no vehicles allowed, just transportation and bikes, and running. I thought this would be a great central spot. We'll get up in the air with the drone and show you all the different quadrants of living because the Portland Metro is ginormous, and it can be kind of confusing where the perfect place to live is. We are constantly being contacted by people relocating here, and we absolutely love it. If you are moving here, relocating here, and you have any questions, reach out to Jesse Dau or me anytime, day or night. Shoot us a text, phone call, or email, and we've got your back.

So, for 'Where to Live in Portland, Oregon, When Moving to Portland, Oregon' would sound something like this:

You're thinking about moving to Portland. You have no idea where to live. I did the same damn thing just a couple of years ago. Well, in this video, we're going to be interviewing Jesse, and we're going to talk about the four major sections of Portland, Oregon. And the best news is you're going to learn a couple of these areas that you might like to live in, but most importantly, a bunch of areas you're going to hate to live in Portland, Oregon. So stay tuned.

Now, as we learn further in this book, negative wins. That's all the news is. Every day it's the five top worst stories in the United States, and that's just what sells. So by putting in, 'you're going to learn a bunch of areas you're going to hate to live in Portland, Oregon,' that gets the viewers to stay forever.

We built our branded intro and made it about the city, instead of about us. I took a bunch of clips of Jesse and vlogging to the beat, and that was our little intro. It just kind of sets the video up, and it was something that had not been done in real estate. It was our brand.

So that's what we did. And the subscribers started growing, the views were growing, I had the hook in there, but I never told anybody to call us. That day at the Tilikum Crossing, when I was waiting for Jesse, and I'm sitting there feeling bad for myself because I ain't closing nothing from these videos, I thought 'I got to try this.' What could I say to get people to call me?

The channel was all about Portland, Oregon, not me. I'm not the top agent. I don't give a shit about that stuff. I got all of that out of my system before now. So, our intro ended up being:

Hey, what's up? This is Jackson Wilkey with the Real Agent Now group right here in the Portland metro. If this is your first time on this channel and you want to learn everything about what it's like to work, eat, sleep, live, and play right here in Portland, then make sure you tap that subscribe button and you click the bell, so you're notified every time we do a new video.

We get calls every day from people moving and relocating to Portland, and we absolutely love it. So if you're thinking about moving anywhere in Portland, Oregon, or Southwest Washington, make sure you give us a call, shoot us a text, send us an email, send us the pigeon carrier. However you want to get a hold of us. We got your back when moving to Portland, Oregon.

Jesse always said "we got your back." So I incorporated that. But that day, I created a call to action of just, *hey, we have a lot of people who are moving, relocating here that reach out to us every day, and we love it. So if you are thinking of moving to Portland, make sure you give us a call. Shoot us a text.* I said that in that video, and the next day, we got 14 phone calls. It was insane. We had this huge built-up audience of people dying for this information, but since we never told them to call, they didn't. The calls were like, "Oh, my God. Thank you so much for telling us to call you. We didn't even know you guys were doing real estate. We just love your videos. They helped us with our move there. Can you help us buy a house?" It was insane.

I had to really invent this YouTube video intro script structure, and it is so pertinent to the success of our YouTube. Now you hear that exact line and calls to action and hooks and everything in everybody's videos. That's fine. Don't change it. It just works. Now you can incorporate your own call to action and change it a little bit. I don't care. But it works. That is where the YouTube hook, intro, call to action, all came from. It was from all of the trials and tribulations before finally figuring out that I need to hook people at the beginning instead of talking about myself, and my open house, and my listing, and my property, and my my my.

If you look at your data in your analytics now, it's rare to get 15- 20% of people to watch the whole video in its entirety. So if you throw your call to action at the end, you're missing out on 80% plus of your traffic, and they're not going to call you. But if you come with the value and say something along the lines of "we get so many people who reach out, and we absolutely love it." People have FOMO now. They cannot wait to reach out. We've had people reach out with eight-year plans to move because of that call to action. You've got to get it in there. One major thing I hear over and over is "Jackson, hey, I'm just starting out a YouTube channel. I can't say that I had calls yet." This is the beautiful part about YouTube. This isn't flash-in-the-pan bullshit like TikTok. This shit works forever. My very first videos are still working for me today, three years later. Hell, they're going to work for my kids. My kids are nine, six, and two. These videos will work for them. I'm going to keep getting a lot of calls with all of our channels. We've had over 15,000 reach outs from either call, text, email, LinkedIn, Facebook message, direct message, and pigeon carriers. I've been called everywhere. You have to have your call to action in there, and you own it right away. This is a platform that's evergreen. If you make killer videos, they work for you the rest of your life. And you're not going to be lying in that video in a couple of months when you have had lots of reach outs. So that is really the game changing element of YouTube.

To this day, handling YouTube is still my favorite thing to do. I manage 13 channels, and I'm constantly in the YouTube studio and the analytics section. I filter down to seven days to see what's been happening in the last week, 28 days to see what's happened last month, and 365 to see what's happened in the last year. It's all in the analytics.

CHAPTER 8

Living in YouTube Channels

"Your income is determined by
how many people you serve and
how well you serve them."

– Bob Burg, The Go-Giver

When we started out, the *Living in Portland, Oregon* Channel was just Jackson Wilkey. It was the first YouTube account I created. The very first video I ever uploaded was a video of my son, Hank, playing with monster trucks. Like any proud father, I thought this super cute vid of my boy was going to go viral, *obviously*. After that, I was going to be a millionaire, and I'd never have to build power lines again in my life. Well, that didn't exactly work. Problem was, I didn't understand YouTube at all. And you know what? It took a long time to figure it out.

That was just my regular YouTube channel. In fact, I don't even love talking about it because it annoys Jesse so much that it was created with my prehistoric Yahoo email account. I even have a video on there about the *Sushi Bazooka*. Yep, that shit is a thing. Not to go too far into detail about what I thought at the time was a pretty nifty device, but it's a thing. And it's a thing that has sweet fuck all to do with real estate. But hey, like I said, you gotta start somewhere.

Now, it's important here to give credit where credit is most definitely due; Jesse is always thinking about big-picture stuff, his mind is always ten steps ahead. He's the one in this partnership who plans for the future. The way I used to rock up to the table was just kind of like, 'I need like three grand here so I can buy some brewski's and some diapers.' Jesse knew that in order to get where we were going, we had to build a brand. A brand is also something that later on we could sell–so, effectively we'd double our profits (or much more). With that, we became the 'Real Agent Now' group.

When we changed the channel name, it meant changing everything. Nowadays you can just go right into your customization tab and swap your channel name to whatever you want. Back then, you had to change your whole Google name, and you're only allowed to do it like two or three times. It was a pain in the ass. However, just like we had to start somewhere (read: home videos about Hank's monster trucks and clearly underrated reviews of the iconic Sushi Bazooka), we needed to keep leveling up. So we changed our YouTube channel name to the Real Agent Now Group with Jackson Wilkey and Jesse Dau.

Leveling up also meant thinking more and more about SEO and the YouTube algorithm. Both Jesse and I are numbers guys, but in different ways. He plans structure and loves analytics from the point-of-view where he can scale. I plan content and love analytics because that shit helps us be better than anyone else in the market.

So, we start getting obsessed with data analytics and I begin to truly understand Search Engine Optimization (SEO). All of a sudden, it hit me: what if we changed the channel name to *Portland, Oregon*? Then maybe it would rank for the city name? As I said before, the arrival at this conclusion came from being on YouTube all the time, searching and watching what other people were doing; watching our analytics and seeing what did and didn't work. Sometimes, when I was on YouTube and searching stuff, entire YouTube channels would pop up, and it wouldn't be that person's name.

Now, I didn't leave Idaho and travel all the way to Portland, Oregon, to be like everyone else. Jesse and I share that fire, he didn't get to where he is by being like everyone else either.

Having said all of that, neither Jesse nor I paid attention to one crucial reality: It's not about you, dude! At the time, my goal was to make the best videos and ranking number one. I wasn't thinking as much about the importance of showing people information they could actually use. We had essentially created a YouTube channel that didn't provide any real value to the viewer. All of the information in it was only about us. And it'd take more than one try to get it right.

Even once we had this realization surfaced, we changed our name to Real Agent Now group with Jackson Wilkey and Jesse. It wasn't supposed to be about us, right? But there it was again, we'd fallen into the same trap. Our *About* section was just as bad. It was all, "I got an MBA, and I went to this school. We're the top agents and have helped with 2.3 billion in sales..." Blah blah blah. Nobody gives a shit.

With successful channels, we were seeing that their About section was most often about helping people. So we tweaked our about section to: "Are you thinking about moving or relocating to Portland, Oregon?" That's what this whole channel is about, doing videos of every square inch of the Portland Metro so that people who are moving there, or in many cases already living there, would have a good understanding of some areas where they might like to live.

Jesse was not a fan of, once again, changing the name. We were going all in on the Real Agent Now brand. In his mind we needed to stick with the brand we had been building. He was right, but our name was still wrong. So, we took the leap one last time and moved from the 'Real Agent Now group with Jackson Wilkey and Jesse' to 'Living in Portland, Oregon in July 2019.' With that one small change, we immediately saw positive effects. The videos instantly started ranking higher and higher.

That was the very start of all these 'Living in' channels that are now all across YouTube. Before then, there was not a single 'living in' channel in the world. We've taught thousands of agents how to set up successful channels, and others have straight-up poached the name, but the 'Living in' became hot shit.

Ever since that first video, I wanted to go viral–I just never thought it'd be an entire channel name and style that'd be the thing that did it. It hit big, and that felt damn good (still does).

Honestly, even though it pisses me off when YouTubers say that they 'suddenly realized' they should change their name to 'Living in [City, State]', I love when people use the name. It's great when people use it, and we actively encourage our students to. It's just not super chill when rando's take full credit for coming up with the whole franchise. Even so, just a few short years into it, and we've seen over a thousand 'Living in' channels across the country.

These are the times when it hits home, if only for a second. Because I'll be honest with you, to this day, I still feel like I haven't done shit. I'm not sitting here gloating like I'm this regal and untouchable YouTube God. I'm telling you all of this so that you know that this is doable. You can do this. Will it be a grind? At first, but you'll get there a helluva lot faster if you take these lessons and skip the mistakes we made at first.

So to see there are thousands of these channels is amazing. It's truly one of the coolest things to know that we've built something by getting our asses kicked so freaking hard and admitting that it didn't come easy. Showing people what did and didn't work. And that teaching is something that has changed lots of people's lives. It took a long time to figure out, but helping me build their businesses while avoiding the pitfalls is why I've given away videos for free for years, not just to hook people. People swipe it; that's fine. It's just cool to see.

Now, a little side note, people always tell me that there's already a 'Living In' channel where they are. That's okay. When I moved to Houston, there were eight of my students with 'Living in Houston, Texas' channels. I still created my own *Living in* channel for Houston. Why? Because nobody ever types in a YouTube search and tries to filter their results by who shot the video first. People click for the titles and thumbnails and they stay for the content. The reason people subscribe is consistently useful content and because they vibe with your unique personality.

You can have 100 *Living in* channels, it's about working to be the best, paying attention to channel art, SEO, what you're shooting and why, and being as unapologetically yourself as humanly possible. If you do want to brand yourself a little bit differently, you can always do a moving-in, moving-to, or a [City] living lifestyle, channel.

A couple of our most successful students started a channel called 'Living in Denver - The Mile High Property Brothers.' They kept the *Living in Denver* to rank well but also found a way to add their own name. I love that. Do what you want. I will say that it's important that YouTube knows exactly what that channel is about, and having it in the title makes life that much easier.

CHAPTER 9

The Setback

This is a pretty quick little story, but while I was writing chapter eight, I said something in there, and it made me remember a story, and I want to get this out there, so it will be quick. But it was a massive setback and a huge mistake. We've had other setbacks in the past, but this was the mother of all of them. It's a mistake that I see other marketers teach and that agents are constantly asking me about so let's just set that shit straight.

So, our YouTube channel starts taking off. At this point we're getting quite a few reach outs, closing some deals–this shit was working. Same time, Jesse's getting prouder and prouder of our accomplishment. He's got the Living in Portland channel on the internet version of speed dial, showing chicks for dates (Jesse, if you're reading this, I'm *kidding* on that last part). But yeah, he was pretty pleased with it and I was too.

One day, after doing his rounds, Jesse says to me "dude, we got to put a budget to this thing." He wanted to run some paid ads on our channel, but I was skeptical. He explained to me that, after adding the CTAs to our vids, we'd been getting a pretty consistent flow of views, subscribers, and calls. Like it started going crazy once we got that call to action there. Jesse was of the mind that it could only help. Makes sense, you'd think that lying down an ad budget would essentially turbo boost our current stats–after all, that's what ads are for. But still, when it came to YouTube, I wasn't convinced. I respond to Jesse with a wary tone, "yo bro, I don't think it's gonna work. In fact, I think it's gonna hurt.

At the time, we had just gone through this whole phase of not sharing our videos on other social media platforms because it messed with our click-through rates and average view durations (not in a good way). My thought on the matter was that ad budget would skew all those numbers even more. Because, here's the thing, once you've paid for ads, the algorithm knows that you've paid and will treat your channel accordingly. Sound like the kind of paranoia reserved only for those who have a Nest camera attached to the front of their house? It might sound like it, but it's not. The algorithm knows.

Still, Jesse wanted to just try it out for a few days–that way, we could target the hottest markets. We had a lot of viewers from California, New York and a few other areas. We talked about it; I let him know that I thought it was a bad idea and he let me know that he wanted to just try it out anyway. And, at the end of the day, we're in a partnership. So, we did it.

If you've ever run Google ads or YouTube ads, you'll know that there's a lot to it. Honestly, I highly recommend not doing it. You'll get tons of marketers saying that it's the play, but it ain't always the play. Especially when it comes to an industry that relies heavily on trust, like real estate. If you do end up wanting to use ads, say for listings, it's good to know that Google and YouTube ads are a billion times better than Facebook ads. But, me? I hate paying for anything. I only want to work with people who found us and decided to call. This approach is twofold: firstly, I don't have to pay shit for getting our name out there, and secondly, the people who find us organically actually *want* to work with us. They did the research, they made the decision, and I truly believe that there's something to that.

But I digress, back to the story. So, I go in and set these suckers up. While Google and YouTube ads are among the best (when you actually do need to use ads), they're also much more intricate than Facebook ads. This, I did not know. So, I do a $10-a-day budget. Ten dollars on YouTube videos tends to equal thousands and thousands of views. We placed the main ad on one of our vlogs. It's one of our best. I do believe it was a 'Where to Live in Portland When Moving There.' As one of our best, this video was the first one we added a call to action to.

It just so happened that the day after hitting play on our new ads, Jesse had a listing appointment. Now, one thing he would do, is that he would go to his listing appointments, pull up the YouTube channel and say something along the lines of 'look at all these subscribers and views we get on a daily basis. I'm gonna get your property out there to all these people.' People undoubtedly loved hearing it. I'd also like to note that he would show off just as much around town, at the bars and all that. We were becoming the highest ranked channel for anything to do with living in Portland, Oregon. Whether it was where to live in general or a video about something like the top five neighborhoods, our videos were ranking number one. So, he's at this listing and he's feeling pretty high and mighty about all the shit we had to show for ourselves. He loved it.

At this point, the ads had been running for like two days. Then he calls me with a "fuck, Jackson. What the hell happened to our YouTube channel?!" He'd gone to pull up our vids and couldn't find them or the channel anywhere. The search results were so barren that he thought I might've erased it all. I didn't think I had, but started to panic. So I haul ass and I go to check. I'm on the computer, logged into the backend of our YouTube, so I can quite clearly see that all of our stuff was still up and running. "Thank god for that," I thought.

Once I'd confirmed everything was still in its rightful place, I go back to Jesse. "I'm telling you, dude, it's that *fucking* budget we did, it's that money." He quickly responded "turn that shit off!" After the whirlwind of destruction they caused within a time period of just 48 hours, I was obviously going to turn them off. Before running the ads, I'd been in two minds about it all. On one hand, I'd had a gut feeling that the ads would have a negative effect, but on the other hand, I was curious. Well, the gut don't lie.

We had taken this video that was killing it organically. Before the ads, it was in front of people who were most likely to watch it. After we attached a budget, this started going out to hundreds of thousands of people. Sounds like a good thing, yeah? Nope. Now if you don't know the difference between views and impressions, impressions mean that they've seen the thumbnail of the video. Whether they are scrolling past it or even hover over it for a while, impressions are not actually that impressive. So, we were getting all the impressions in the world. But what we were not getting was clicks. We probably got *some* clicks, and I'm sure we got some views out of it as well. But that doesn't mean a goddamn thing if the people who are clicking and viewing aren't actively interested in what you have to say. For instance, we were getting put in front of real estate agents that were likely just looking due to curiosity.

The second thing this wonderful experiment did was to our YouTube channel as a whole. It pulled literally everything out of ranking. It crushes your channel. Our videos went out to hundreds of thousands of people across the country and they did not give two shits about that video because *they didn't search for it*. It was put in their laps. Like I mentioned, yes, we probably got some views out of it, but it tore our channel up. Our average view duration of our channel plummeted. Our click-through rates fell through the floor. All the key ranking indicators of a video, shot.

I will never attach a budget again. I get emails on the daily from people who want to start running YouTube ads. The thought being that it'll be their channel (new or established), but on steroids. They're gonna get all these views, all these clicks. Except, they're not going to. You gotta let these things go organic.

It is so difficult to watch your stats on a new channel because you might only get three views or six views or ten views. But honestly, that is 100% better. I've said it millions of times; I would rather have three views from people who searched and found my content and watched that video for a longer period of time than pay for millions of views that do nothing. Those three views I got are going to carry this channel and help me crush it for a long freaking time. Paying and forcing content kills your channel. That's why you don't get business from your ads. Nobody searched for content like yours and found it. 9.5 times outta 10, your videos did not provide any value to the person who clicked an ad. Therefore you're not getting business from it.

If I can help you in any way, I'd advise that you do not share your videos from YouTube to other Facebook groups and do not attach a budget. I've grown 13 channels, I know how painful it is to watch a new channel try to grow. It takes weeks if not months for it to really get going, but I promise you it'll work 10 times better in the long run if you allow them to rank organically. Now you might be saying, 'well Jackson, you can attach a budget to some videos. And, yes, that works for some videos, like listings. I suggest that you create a separate brand account, separate videos, and do it that way. I would not even do it on your channel. They say if you unlist the video, then it doesn't hurt your channel. I call bullshit. I've been staring at channel analytics for a long time now, and the numbers will show you how much running ads can instantly nuke your channel. Create a brand account. It takes about five seconds, and you can run ads off that channel all you want. Don't do it to your high-performing organic videos. You work so hard to get these good long organic videos going. It'll just tear them down by sharing them in real estate Facebook groups or attaching a budget.

CHAPTER 10

The Partner Fight

I remember a time when I was feeling a lot lower than Jesse was. He was on cloud nine, and I really had some serious internal struggles going on. It's not like me to talk about emotions or bring anything up; I am a person that will just hide from any kind of confrontation. I'm too nice. In fact, I've got a coach now, and we talk about this regularly. One of my biggest faults is just allowing people to walk all over me. I'm not saying Jesse was doing that, he wasn't, but just saying that in general, that's what I'll do. I'll just hide from confrontation. At the time, I really had some things burning inside of me, and I finally got the courage to talk to Jesse about it, and I will tell you, it was crazy and it led to a lot of tears.

I think this chapter will be relatable to a lot of people, not just in the YouTube world but in general. First of all, having a partner in real estate, to be honest, is probably the best thing that you can possibly do. The biggest mistake we've seen is that people like to choose other partners who are just like them. So they do everything the same. You have two of the same personality, and when they're getting along, it's amazing. But you also start to realize you don't get shit done. Because what a true partnership means is 'hey, you're going to do the stuff that I don't want to do, or I don't know how to do.' Fortunately for Jesse and I, our brains, personalities, and heighths (he's going to kill me for that one), are all 180° out. We are completely different humans. If we were the same, we'd never get shit done. I have certain ways of getting stuff done; it frustrates Jesse. He does amazing work at structuring teams and promoting us, and it drives me crazy. And that's what was happening when our partnership first started. I didn't know how to handle his personality. I didn't know that the dude is basically a modern-day Don King, but of sales. He was promoting us, but sometimes the way that he was doing it was really affecting me. It felt as if he was taking the majority of the credit, and it really bothered me.

So this chapter is really about how to find a partner, how to keep each other focused on the goal, and communicate. Well, how we did it. Since that fight, we've had conversations where I bawled my eyes out to him and had so much shit going on in the house and the family, and he's like, "You got to come to me more with this stuff." Then there are times where he's just getting his ass kicked, and I know exactly where he's at, so I can help him through it. Jesse and I are grinders. I talked about this in another chapter, but I still feel like I haven't done anything in this YouTube world. That's where my focus is. Having somebody along the ride who can do all the things that you can't is so pivotal to success.

Up till this chapter, this dude has been basically paying my bills. I'm doing all the videos, I'm doing the YouTube stuff, and he's actually closing deals. I always have to remember that. But let's dive into this partner fight. We started having success finally. Now the reach outs are coming in thick and fast and we actually had some closed deals. I don't remember exactly where we were in the time frame of the whole YouTube real estate thing because it was just really moving quickly, but Jesse was promoting us everywhere. "We're the greatest," "we're the number one," "we're top everything." My personality is not that way, I'm more of a kind of 'I'll hide back and just do my thing. I'll be the happy-go-lucky guy.' The loud communication via social media is not the way I communicate. So it kind of rubbed me the wrong way. I'll be brutally honest because I had a lot of people reaching out to me via social media and saying things like, 'Dude, when is Jesse going to stop talking about all this stuff? He's in everybody's face, and he's loud, and he's brash.' It bothered me, so I knew where they were coming from. With that validation, it got into my head. I'm hoping this relates to you in some way. If anything or anybody gets in your head, you have to realize who people are and what their intentions are.

When you're working with somebody who has a mind like Jesse, you come to learn that he's ten steps ahead at all times. He knew what he was doing back then. I had no idea. He knew that by putting all this daily content, showing off our successes, and getting literally everything out there, it would lead to a lot of attention for us. But, when you get to the point where you're frustrated, there's nothing anybody can do or say. You flip the narrative to where everything somebody does is negative. I was at that point, and his posts started coming off as if it was *his* real estate team, and *his* YouTube channel, and *his* ideas. Meanwhile, I spent every day entrenched in YouTube. That's all I did. I'm not making this up–I spent 10 hours a day studying YouTube, watching videos, editing videos, shooting videos, and getting our content to rank. I would tell Jesse all these groundbreaking things that I'm teaching you in this book and that I've taught for 3+ years. All this stuff I've given away for free through the pain of learning, and yet he would boast about it via Facebook, Instagram, and YouTube. In my mind, I felt like he was taking credit for all of it.

I got to a point where I felt like I was done. I was going to find somebody else to close deals because I couldn't take it anymore. I truly feel like he was taking all the credit. This is actually really hard to talk about. I was planning on doing the videos, and instead of this guy taking all the credit, I was going to find someone else to partner with. Thank God I never did.

Like I said, it has always been difficult for me to talk about my emotions. However, I know that by being raw and authentic on podcasts, videos, and this book, it helps so many agents. If you're at this point, talk to your partner or your wife or your husband. I have to do this now with my wife. When we're frustrated with each other, we're both just never going to see eye to eye. But when we start communicating, we usually find out that we basically want the exact same thing. I'm actually looking in the camera right now while saying all this, and looking back at myself like, "Jackson, you need to do this more."

I grew up in a family where my parents lived together, what they thought was for the kids, but yet they showed no affection. They didn't love each other. I don't know if they loved each other. But there was no affection. There was no hugging. There was nothing they did together. They only stayed together for us. It taught me that the whole affection and communication thing wasn't important. It's something that I'm working on right now and definitely doing with my kids.

This is going a little bit deeper, but I'm hoping that it helps you because everybody gets frustrated at some point. You're going to go to a point where you're just going to want to give up on that person. If you just open up, tell them how you're feeling, and just get it out there, you may be surprised at the reaction. It took me 37 years to confront the emotions I was feeling toward my parents. I sent them an eleven-minute video to tell them how I felt. I thought it was just going to rock them, but to my surprise, they both thanked me and admitted that it's a conversation that should've happened long before. It has opened up this new line of communication with my parents. It is one of the greatest things ever. We're having meaningful conversations. It feels so good. For thirty-seven years, I held that in. Now that it's out in the open, we see each other more, we talk more, and there's affection. And now, I get to teach my kids this.

One day Jesse and I were downtown by his condo, in the Pearl District, and we were talking YouTube. The whole time, I was seething. I couldn't hear a word he was saying. It reminds me of when I was going to propose to my wife. She could have been talking about having 7 boobs or 37 toes or something, and I wouldn't have heard what she was saying. With Jesse that day, I can't tell you one word he said, and I remember him being in a great mood. Like at this point, things are moving, things are shaking, we're getting all this attention, and shit is actually finally working. For Jesse, that's all he wants–he just wants stuff that works without blatantly wasting his time. He had invested a lot of time and money into everything we were doing. He believed in me, and thank God he continued to, but this day was the breaking point. In my mind, he was taking all the credit and I was doing all the work. Now, I couldn't have been more wrong, but at that time, I was going crazy every day and night. All the long hours we put in also meant that I was missing time with my kids, which is my biggest pet peeve. It goes back to me being a lineman, and missing birthdays, holidays, nights, and weekends. It's kinda like a PTSD thing for me. So when I started missing out on family time and events, that was the other effect it was having on me. I was pissed.

So, I'm sitting and I finally say to Jesse "Dude, I got to say something. I've been seeing all your social posts lately, and I swear to you, it feels like you're taking credit for all this. It's your real estate team. It's your YouTube channel. It's your everything. Dude, I feel like you're just leaving me in the dust." At first, he was like, "What the fuck do you mean? Are you fucking kidding me?" But he's smart, too. Very smart. He broke down into tears, he was shaking. And when Jesse gets to that kind of emotion, he looks down at the ground. You can just see his mind spinning. He was just like, "Jackson, you mean more to me than anyone." Honestly, I'm crying right now, just recalling this story. I'm an emotional dude. Jesse went on to say, "dude, I literally talk about you more than anybody I know. I want more for you, man. I want more for you and your kids, than anybody on this planet. I think the fucking world of you, dude. You're the best partner in the world." When he did that and opened up and cried, I lost my shit and started crying too. Jesse continued on to say "Dude, I'm doing this for a bigger picture, but don't ever for one second think that I don't appreciate you. You're the best thing that happened to me, man. Nobody else understands. They are on the outside looking in. So let them create their own vision, we have ours." And guess what, guys? It was nipped in the bud that very day. And guess what it did to me? It fired me up. I had more motivation. I was going to take us further. Nowadays, I love how Jesse posts on social media. It's just who he is. If you know him and you follow him long enough, you'll know that he doesn't give two shits. He's going to put everything out there. He's not going to put a bunch of fluff. At the end of the day, he was the Don King of sales, and he still is.

Yes, I've put out the majority of the content about YouTube for real estate and figured a lot of this stuff out, but I wouldn't be anywhere if it weren't for him. The whole business side of this; just would have fallen through the cracks. I've coached agents who are like me; they're great on video, but they can't close a single deal, not one. Some will even have 100 reach outs, and you might be sitting here listening to me going, 'how the hell do you have 100 reach outs, and you don't close deals?!' Our brains just don't work that way. I lived off of sticky notes and zero communication and even less follow-up. I am so entrenched in YouTube and the video thing. Work-wise, that's all I've loved and cared about. I needed a guy like that to not only close these deals but someone I can communicate with like we do. Whether you think it's Brash or not, Jesse was, and always is, speaking the truth.

That was one of the hardest but best times in our partnership. Since then, we're way more open to each other, and we've still had times where either one of us needs to talk but just keeps putting it off. But when we sit down and talk, we're on the same page, and you would not believe the motivation that comes out of that. We're just ready to go. Jesse and I will go to war for each other, we'll do anything for each other. I'm going to focus on my strengths, and he's going to focus on his. We'll look each other in the eye and say,

'I fucking hate doing X, Y, and Z, and I'm never doing it again.' When you tell Jesse that, he goes, 'Thank you. Perfect. I will find a virtual assistant, and we will hire that out. Anything that you ever don't want to do, you let me know, and we will hire that out.' I feel like I'm the video guy and have to do it all. And now, I got VAs and executive assistants, and it really comes down to this guy understanding the business aspect of it and us having open communication.

Our whole goal is to help people with free, organic information and if we can't help you with the free organic stuff, if it's too hard, then we'll build out some systems that can help you. Our ultimate aim is to help as many people as we possibly can. We've had tons of emails from agents. Some of my absolute favorites are from agents who have been in the game for years, telling us that we've helped them make doing real estate fun again. Not having to cold call and reach out to family and friends. Now these people have clients reaching out to them, wanting to work with them specifically.

Our partner fight truly changed the trajectory of our Channel Junkies brand, because it may not have been here today had I not said something and had Jesse not opened up. When he talked about my family and me, and when he put my family first, that's when I knew this is the dude for me, and that's what made me go 10x. To this day, we've continued going full steam ahead. Hundreds and hundreds of free videos, free webinars, and teachings. I mean, I love it. I'm up for helping every single person I can with their real estate business, from video marketing and doing it right to avoiding doing all the shit that doesn't work. It's my absolute passion, and I'm so so glad that I have Jesse.

CHAPTER 11

I Hate Being Hated

There's a way that you can attract dream clients; by being absolutely hated, and nobody in the YouTube world for real estate has more haters than your boy Jackson Wilkey. So in this chapter, I want to talk about haters. I also want to start talking about how hard YouTube was at the beginning. Not only was I figuring out how to do YouTube and read the data, but–what I know now to be the hardest part about YouTube–I was learning how to be myself. Now, I coach thousands of agents, and if you have ever had a coaching call with me, you'll usually there's not a lot of just magical 'do this, do that. Here's the perfect title.' I'm literally coaching you on how to be you.

I hate being hated. Going back to high school, I was always the nice guy. I had this buddy named Jonah; a super nice kid, funny as can be. He got picked on by other people, but I was always nice to him. I loved my Jonah man. He was hilarious. But one day he wrote me a note. My mom saw it and she said,

"This is the proudest I've ever been of you." Among other things, the note from Jonah said "I just really want to thank you for always being cool to me." I also had my buddies, Nick and Sarah. They both had Down Syndrome and were as awesome as can be. I graduated in 2002. S Club 7 was a popular band back then, and Nick thought he was in S Club 7. Hell, he was in S Club 7. He told me I could be in the band and now it's S Club 8. Sarah was the greatest, she nicknamed me 'Woogey' because she found it hard to pronounce Wilkey. She came into the lunchroom one day screaming "Woogey! Woogey! Woogey!!" and the nickname stuck after that.

One day I was at my locker, and Sarah comes up behind me. "Sarah, what are you doing?" I said. "I'm getting in my locker," she responds. "That's not your locker, Sarah. I've been here for two months, you have never had your locker there." She's like, "No, I'm getting in my locker. I got a locker right by you." I didn't know how she could've after two months, so I say "Sarah, knock it out. You don't have a locker right there." *Chink*. She opens this thing. She ended up getting a locker right next to me and we got to hang more often.

I say this not to say that I'm the greatest person ever, but I am nice to people. I hate being mean to people, and I hate being hated. Now I'm about to get real with you. As a kid, I had a pretty wild imagination. I hate being hated so much that a lot of times, especially growing up, I would always try to be someone else. I also loved the attention. I understand there are a lot of you out there that are the polar opposite, and that's just fine because who you are is who you are.

Back in middle school and high school, when windup cameras or digital cameras hit the scene, I was all over that stuff. I was all about that attention. If I saw someone, whether an actor, rapper, or just someone who I thought was cooler than me, I had this urge to become them. In 9th grade, I went through this phase where I rocked a 'No-Limit' chain. Yeah, I was BAD AF. Basketball was my jam, no doubt. Then junior year hit, and I started just crushing beers and hanging out with the older crew, the loggers and miners, and I totally transformed into a full-blown hick.

Now I got a hick Southern accent, and I'm from Idaho, sounding like I'm from Mississippi or something. I've just always had this in me that I had to be something else. I had to be somebody else and sound different to be cool, right? That's what I thought. And that's what I repeatedly kept shooting myself in the foot with.

When we first started creating our content, I tried to emulate other agents I'd seen on YouTube. At the time, as long as they were on video, I thought they were obviously cooler than me. So I would sound the way they sounded, I would look the way they looked. It really put me behind schedule and made me extra critical of myself. This is also back when I was editing everything, so I had control. So if I saw something that I didn't like, which was usually just me being myself, I edited that shit out. If you watch my earlier videos, it's jump cut after jump cut. I took every pause, every 'um,' every break and I cleaned that shit up. I thought it had to be perfect.

At the time, I had no idea that I was hustling backward. I was straying so far away from myself that I was never going to attract my ideal client. But you can also hear a little bit of both of my high school identities because I might say 'son of a bitch,' 'hell yeah,' 'grab me a brewski,' and you might also hear me say things like, 'what up, homies? Yeah, I keep it ghetto country. Point is, you really can't be anyone other than who you are. You can act like someone else, you can pick little ticks or sayings up along the way, but you'll never find your people by acting like someone else.

In the last chapter, when I talked about the partner fight, you can see how different Jesse and I are.. If you waste his time, fuck you, dude. He is so direct, and I am a people person. And we never would've found how good we are at working together if we were pretending to be people we aren't.

So imagine getting into a world now where you're displaying your personality in front of 10 people in the start, and then 50 people, and then 1000 people, and then collectively, millions of people. They get to judge me quickly, and often anonymously. The security of being behind a screen and not having to talk shit to someone's face means that people (trolls) really amp that shit up sometimes. I always felt like I had to defend myself in these comments. At first, I was a comment warrior. I literally scoured every single day, every comment that came in, and I felt like I had to sit there and defend myself, and it made me change who I was on video all the time. When they would comment about how loud or obnoxious I was, in the next video, I'd be a little bit quieter. If they said I moved around too much, the next time, I would try and hold still, and if I saw myself moving, I would stop and reshoot it. They got into my head. I was trying to please everybody.

In my mind, I'm doing this video thing and now I'm getting blown up with negative comments. On Facebook, it was all positive because it was all real estate agents worshiping each other's content. Then when I got into the real world of YouTube, and it was actual people searching and finding my content. And, let me tell you, some pretty fucking weird people come out of the woodworks; tinfoil hat-wearing, in their mom's basement, people who just shred you. I swear, some people spend the majority of their day surfing videos just to talk shit. It was tough, and one of the toughest ones was, after my third channel in North Idaho, somebody *actually* started a Facebook group against my partner and I. The person started it because he wanted to 'keep Idaho, Idaho.' Seriously? Towns in Northern Idaho are small town and redneck-as-it-gets. That's where I was born and raised, and here's this dude who creates a Facebook group and posts our videos in there, and everybody's commenting shit like, 'these are the people ruining Idaho.'

I ended up knowing who the guy was. This fake ass mother trucker had relocated to Idaho seven years before. Like, are you kidding me? I got the birth certificate, homie. That shit rocked me. So it wasn't like I got over it right away. Even today if I see something, it's a hard pill to swallow. People often ask, "Do you monitor your comments to get people to reach out to you?" My answer today is, "Hell, no." All of our channels together get around 200-400 comments a day, and I don't read them. I've had 15,000+ reach outs. If people want to get a hold of me, they'll get a hold of me. If they're kicking tires and only hanging out in the comments, they're probably worse than a Zillow lead. I don't want to go in there and ruin my day. I'm too nice of a guy, and I hate being hated.

I've been told by many that I'm ruining states. Idaho is the perfect example. Loads of people 100% blame me for ruining Idaho–for too many people moving there. They truly feel that my YouTube videos are what's driving all these people to Idaho. As if I'm running advertisements that call out Idaho as the greatest place to live. No, Idaho has been a place where people move to so they can have their guns, hunt and fish since the 60s. In 2002, it was the hottest market in the country with the number one fastest growing economy. But yet, when I started YouTube videos 21 years later, I was the problem. It really affected me. It made me want to quit.

It was even harder to deal with the naysayers when I first got started in the Portland real estate scene. Every damn day I'd have agents throwing it in my face that I wasn't good enough, saying stuff like 'put in your time. I'm the top agent. I've been doing this for 20 years.' Or when I was cold calling, doing open houses and knocking on doors. You're trying to convert people, and then they ask the dreaded question, 'how many deals have you done? How long have you been in real estate?' So, you know what? I started becoming the top local agent in all my videos. I wore my fucking name tag. I had my dress-up pants. I had my perfect sweater on. As far as everyone else was concerned, I was a Portland local and I was a top real estate agent. That's what you had to be–you had to be something that you weren't. So now I had to shoot these YouTube videos for people moving to Portland, and I had to be the Portland local. If I'm not a local, they're not going to trust me. If they didn't trust me, they were going to hate me.

So I'm shooting all these videos early on, talking about all these areas I love. Before I actually knew the areas, I would read up on them, or I would ask people. I'd act like I've been there forever, and I love doing this, but was really making it all up. If you look at my earlier videos, you'll notice I was wearing dress shoes, dress shirts, dress pants, and as soon as I turned that damn camera off, I took that shit right off. I hated it. Shirts and buttons are so confining, and I definitely hate dress shoes. That's why I now live in the south, because there's a noticeable lack of snow. Now I wear shorts, casual shoes and t-shirts all day, and that's how I feel most confident and comfortable.

At one point, I realized something had to change. Yes, we're getting more attention and starting to get comments every once in a while. People would say things like 'oh, my gosh, I can't believe you said that' or 'that brewery that you were talking about seems amazing.' After a minute of that, it all clicked. These people are actually listening to my words and they like the same stuff I like. They liked the way I acted in the off moments where they caught a glimpse of me being real. I didn't know this at the beginning but now teach people to be themselves. Trust me, I know every single one of you is going, 'I don't know how to be myself' or 'what do you mean?' And yep, it's very difficult. Trust me. It took me even longer. I didn't have anybody coaching me on how to be myself.

At this point, you have to realize too, that the entire real estate industry was predicated on market updates, escrow, inspection, and being the top local agent. Every single real estate video you watched then and even today, you see, 'hi, my name is such and such, your local agent. I've been in the market 20 years.' After trying all that and it not working, I thought "Fuck it. I'm going against everybody."

I decided at one point that I was going to do this video called 'Moving to Portland, Oregon, My Story.' And it went a little something like this:

So you're thinking about moving to Portland, Oregon. I just did it a couple of years ago. In this video, I'm going to teach you exactly what I went through during my first few years of living in Portland, Oregon. So stay tuned.

[music break]

What's up, everybody? This is Jackson Ray Wilkey. Where's Jesse? But yes, it's just me this week. So I wanted to shoot some videos about what it's like to live and move to Portland because I did it myself just a couple of years ago. Alright, so I thought it would be fun to just kind of talk to you about my experience of moving here just a couple of years ago with a family of four and a wiener dog. This is the Brew dawg. He came with us. And now, we're expecting our third child at the end of the month. So we'll go over how this family of four, turning into five, and a wiener dog did when moving to Portland, Oregon.

The reason I wanted to do this video, and basically out myself for A.) not being a Portland local and B.) being a new agent, was that I started understanding what people wanted. The comments *tell* you what they like. The metadata and traffic sources show you what people are searching for. The comments are straight from the horse's mouth and the data don't lie. There were things I understood about Portland that Jesse didn't understand because he was born and raised there. I realized that people were really enjoying that aspect. So I think I told Jesse, ", I'm going to do this video called 'Moving to Portland, Oregon – My Story' I don't know if this is going to make or break us, but I'm just going to talk about my story. So people are going to now know that I'm new here and that I'm a new agent, too, obviously."

So I did this video, talked about some of the areas we'd lived in, what it was like moving there and why my family chose to live there. Also, why we decided to move there in the first place. If you fully read chapters 1 and 2, you already know that I just needed to get away from my small town. Portland, to me, is a massive town. It has so many opportunities. There's corporate structure with big brands like Nike and Intel. There are good schools there and way more things to do, etc. Then I started talking about things that caught me off guard. How Portland can be almost impossible to get around. The traffic is some of the most brutal I've ever seen because this city is so old, and there are mountains, lakes, and rivers everywhere, so they can't expand these highways. It's kind of screwed. The one thing that drove me nuts when moving here was daycare costs and even finding decent daycare that was enrolling. In Idaho, I was paying $42 a day for two kids to go to daycare. In Portland, that number rose to $56 a day for one kid. We ended up putting my son into kindergarten a year early because it was more affordable than putting him into daycare. He's a summer baby, so it worked out. Another issue was that I couldn't get to school in time to pick them up, so we had to bus them to this after-school program for 30 minutes a day. And they charged $36 every day! So I'm into this at a 100 bucks a day, and I am dead ass broke. That was at first. Then, after being there for a year and a half, we got chatting to coworkers, friends, and neighbors. From that, we discovered that there are these little side daycares that take 10-12 kids and they're $30- $40 a day. But they can also be really hard to get into. So, in the video, I told people to make sure they lock in daycare before moving to Portland.

So I shot this thing, and immediately, it became one of our top-performing videos. Reach-outs, comments, views; everything was buzzing. We've probably had 100+ people reach out and about the daycare and how it took them forever to get. The first lady that reached out said:

Jackson, that video you did about moving there hit me so hard. Thank you so much for that. We've never found any kind of videos like that, and it's prepared us so much more for our move to Portland, and we're really excited. That thing you said about daycare, you were right. It took us three months to find one for our kids. So I just really want to thank you from the bottom of my heart for doing that because we would have been screwed. But my family and I, we are moving there. We have a budget of $600,000 to $700,000. Could you help us find a home?

That's when I realized, I did it. I made that shit happen, finally. It made sense, too. If somebody had said to me, before or when I moved to Portland, 'Hey, man, I moved to Portland too, now I help people move, relocate, and show you all the things that you're going to not know.' I would have been like, "What's your fucking number? Because I'm calling you right now."

Now, you might be sitting here thinking that you can't make *Moving to* style videos because you were born and raised in your area. You know what, you can. And as you dig in more and work with people moving there, you'll start to understand their pain points. I now understand what people don't get about Idaho, things that I took for granted my whole life.

On our Idaho channel, I tell people about that stuff, and I also talk about the wrong areas to move to in Idaho. "Do you realize in Spirit Lake, on Highway 53, there's a snow belt? If you don't like snow, first and foremost, don't move to Idaho. I've seen it snow in May. I've seen it snow in June." But how is that going to attract anybody? Especially people from Arizona or California, where they've spent their whole lives warm. Sometimes, when you've grown up in one environment, you want to move to a different one. They may want to ski, snowboard, or maybe even just have the opportunity to make snow angels when the moment strikes them.

I'm living in Texas now because I'm so sick and tired of the snow. I wanted something different. I was just on the phone with my mom today. It's the middle of June and yesterday was 40°. It was hailing and almost snowing. I'm tired of that shit. But when I talk local, I talk about these things. I'll tell people to make sure they get a house with a wood stove, and always have two or three cords of wood on hand. Cords of wood are $250 a piece, and 2-3 of them will take you through the winter. Or I'll tell them if they live in such and such an area, they're going to have rocks the size of Dodge Neon, but people out there love it. You got five acres, you can shoot guns, you can dig holes, you can do whatever.

Going back to being hated, I learned in the *Moving to Portland* video that being myself wasn't so bad after all. I immediately threw away the nice clothes, the button-ups–I don't even own any of that stuff anymore. We flipped the script entirely. I started wearing t-shirts, shorts, and was often rocking a pair of Air Force Ones. One day, my son, our lender; Addy Nett, and I were doing a Vlog together in Portland's Hollywood district. The opening of that video is all three of us wearing Air Force Ones, and we laid it down with hip hop beats. Then I jump up and do the heel click thing in the air. We got some funny videos of my son eating ice cream, and some shots of Addy and me by a graffitied-up wall. That was our new brand. That was our style from then on. And that's when shit started popping. We started unapologetically being ourselves. We loved it.

The craziest part about our videos before was that Jesse and I tried to be the other person. I was trying to be a local Portland dude. He was trying to talk about family areas. Things we each knew nothing about. As we started opening up, we began understanding what people wanted to know. As our boy Ryan Strong always says, people want to know about these areas, who lives there, who doesn't, and how it's going to help them. So we started loosening up, and I started admitting when I'd never been to an area. We'd be discovering it with people but through the eyes of someone who can appreciate a nice neighborhood and know the different house styles.

My wife, the kids and I took every weekend exploring Portland, and then I would tell the stories of what that area and our experience was like. That honesty attracted more clients than we could ever imagine. I started getting so confident with just being the new guy or just chatting about these areas. People don't care that this city was founded in 1871. They just don't. They don't care about the inspection process. They don't care about the market update. They're moving and have no idea which area would fit them best. You need to answer *those* questions. Whatever your stories are like, whoever you are, it's okay. You'll attract other people, and those people will be ones that match you.

So, we shot a *Living in Portland* style video with Jesse as the host. It was a minute and a half long, and it was the most brutal thing I'd ever listened to. It was terrible. He was really bad at a video when we started. As Jesse started opening up, I asked him about a badass house he'd recently sold to an investor. He loves those topics. So I said "why don't you talk about that?" You see Jesse's eyes light up. And when I got to ask him questions regarding the stuff that he cared about; investor stories, luxury listings, top neighborhoods, best restaurants; Jesse went on and on. You couldn't shut him up, and he had some killer stories. The subjects interested him, that's who he is and that's what this chapter has been all about. Being who you are is the only way to get ahead.

We started figuring out our video partnership. We decided that I'd focus on the family stuff and Jesse would focus on the higher-end neighborhoods, luxury properties, and investments. And he was damn good at it. He'd tell people everything they needed to know to move to Portland's high-end neighborhoods, where the modern homes were, good spots to invest in or get in early. And his videos started blowing up, because he was being himself and his knowledge fit the criteria of people who were listening.

We started attracting these ideal people, and I learned that by being hated, I was loved by my dream clients. Now, everybody that I've ever helped with YouTube all say the same damn thing 'Oh my God, these are the best real estate clients ever.' One girl even said, "Jackson, these YouTube clients are a million times better than referrals." Referrals were the golden standard, but a referral is somebody that you do not know, and you still have to convert. She continued to say "I literally got a referral from a friend the other day, and it was the most awkward thing. I'm used to working with YouTube clients who come in and just love and worship me because they've already filtered me out, and now my friend's friend I'm trying to convert? It was awkward. We really didn't get along that well." It kinda made me realize the same thing, I didn't want to deal with referrals anymore either.

In the spirit of being human, I started putting my kids in the videos. I was so broke to start off with that I couldn't always have them in daycare during the summer. So, instead of juggling, I got them to help me out. And they loved it.

Who would have thought that by putting my kids in the videos, it would have blown us up even more.

People loved seeing Hank and Whit in these videos, and I got some of the coolest intros ever of my kiddos being silly, eating ice cream, sticking their tongues out, and generally having a good time. I had humanized myself, shown people that I was normal.

I also had to take my kids on tours. One day I had Hank with me. At this time, he was about five. He's sitting in the back, probably got his monster trucks, and these people come in. I don't quite know what they look like, and if you've had YouTube clients, you know what this is like. They know who you are. They're waving and saying, "Hey, Jackson. Oh my God." And I'm like, oh, they must be YouTube clients. They're like, "Oh my gosh, it's Hank! What's up, Big Hank?" He's looking at these people like he just saw a ghost. Like, 'Dad, why do these people know me? What in the hell is going on?' I'll never forget it. He was a celebrity. And that's the coolest thing in the world. Something my kids will remember forever.

But I will say those people never ended up buying a house. In fact, I did a lot of tours for people who didn't buy a house. You might be like, well, that doesn't sound that great, guys. We've closed 450+ homes but we had to figure some things out. We do get a lot of people who just want to see areas, and we were getting a lot of our time wasted. But I hate being hated, so I took every YouTube client on the longest tours all day. After all, I had finally cracked the code and I would do anything for them. That's when Jesse told me my time is valuable and we have to tell people that they get 2 hours max. To me, I'm like, 'you gotta be kidding me. No, no, no, I can't do that. They'll hate me.' However, when I did start telling people that I only had 2 hours, they would thank me a ton for setting aside those 2 hours. Setting a boundary worked better than I could've ever imagined.

CHAPTER 12

We Couldn't Close Shit

In a million years, I'll never forget my first YouTube call. But before I get into that, I had a Zillow client. We can all attest to the Zillow client. The brokerage that we were first with was in the beta test of Zillow Flex, and it yielded the worst leads ever. You didn't have to pay for these leads, you just closed them, and you had to pay a referral fee at closing, or whatever it was. I used to love these because I didn't have to prospect–people were calling me. They were like those leads where someone would call and say, 'Hey, I'm actually standing here at this property right now. I'm interested in it.' But this client went one step further, "Hey, I was thinking about taking a chainsaw and cutting my house in half because my wife and I are divorced, and she wants half. Then I'm just going to sell my half, buy 100 acres, put up a bunch of igloos and tents and build an RV camp there." Out of my mind because I was broke as all hell and had never closed a deal, I said to this dude, "Hell, yeah, let's do this. Let's make it happen." I called Jesse and said, "I got a lead. This dude is going to chainsaw his house in half, and it's all going to work perfectly." He's like, "Jackson, you're a fucking idiot. You can't do that." And that was the kind of Zillow clients I was dealing with.

So I'm driving, and I had been touring this chainsaw guy for weeks, looking at all these houses. This is way pre-covid, so this is back in the day when houses actually sat on the market for like 30 days or longer. We would go from house to house to house. The next week I was driving to meet dude at one of those houses, and my phone rang. I looked down at it, and it said *Toronto, Canada*. I thought it was weird but this was before the spam calls had really taken off. So I answered it: "Hello, this is Jackson. Like The Jackson?" I confirmed. He went onto say, "Oh, my God, honey, it's actually him. He answered the phone. I can't believe it's him." It was the first one of these calls, so it came off as pretty strange at the time, but I went with it and asked, "Wait, what's going on?" He continues "we're in Canada. We've been watching your YouTube videos, and we're planning on moving to Portland." At this point, I was thinking, *get the fuck out of here*. I'm emotional, I'm smiling ear-to-ear because I'd heard of people getting calls from their YouTube channels, but now it's real. It was really happening. It had been months, and I quit a few times, and here's the freaking reach out I'd be hoping for. So I pull over, and I'm talking to these people. This dude ends up being just like me, about my age with two kids, wife, and he loves beers. How great is this?! I talked to him for about an hour. Meanwhile, that Zillow client is at this house, I texted him something about being in a traffic jam, I don't know. As you could've guessed, that Zillow client never bought a damn thing from me. Wasted all my time. So I made the right choice in talking to these folks instead. They were planning a trip in a few months to come up and start looking at Portland. Somewhat still in shock, I call Jesse, "you will never believe this… I finally got a call from YouTube." Confused, he says "What?" Barely able to contain my excitement, I said "dude, it freaking finally happened." This was before we had the calls to action in there. So yes, you can still get calls without a call to action, but when you put in the one I created, you'll get 100 million times more reach-outs. But this was the first call, and Jesse was jacked up. I was jacked up. Jesse goes straight into business mode. "Awesome. When are they coming?" I said, "a couple of months, I think." He's like, "Well, what are the dates?" I'm like, "I don't know, a couple of months." He's ready to ask more questions (that I hadn't asked), "Nice, dude. What's their price point?" And I said, "I don't know." He asked, "Are they pre-approved?" I'm like, "I don't know." "What the fuck you mean you don't know?" So I told him, "I don't know. We just sat there and talked. I talked to him for an hour. This dude is like my best friend." Jesse's response said it all, "Jesus. All right, well, reach back out to him, text him, and ask him a few of those questions." So I did and got all the info we needed.

When Jesse told me that he was going to give me 20% of his business, we agreed that it would stay that way until the video thing equals or surpasses what his business bought in. After that, we would go 50-50.

Jesse did 24 deals in his first year and 30 his second. He's very freaking busy, and he had a lot of clients and a lot of real estate going on. So, my job was to do all the videos and work with those clients. So I did.

When we started, I was doing all the tours and answering all the phone calls. Gladly answering these phone calls, by the way, because it meant that I wasn't the one doing the calling. Then the tours started. At first, I did all of them. I answered the calls, I set up the tours, and it was amazing. One time this girl calls; she was moving because she was a nurse, and was trying to decide between Vancouver and Portland. She was staying in downtown Portland at a hotel. I picked her up from the hotel with her luggage and we drove around all day. I showed her the west side of Portland, the areas that I knew. I didn't know many, but the West Side, Beaverton, and Hillsboro. Then she wanted to see Vancouver. So we drove all the way over to Vancouver, and I showed her a ton of neighborhoods. After a full day, she thanked me up and down. We had a great time. Then she flew away, and I never heard from her again.

I had another couple from Las Vegas, this time with a much bigger budget, $600,000-$800,000. He did real estate, apparently. I actually don't know if that was true or not. But they were looking at a little high-end neighborhood in Lake Oswego. They were also interested in some of the new highrise condos downtown. I toured them all day and even went to dinner with them. Next, we went downtown because they needed to go get some snacks. It took them to

Whole Foods, and they were in there for a good 30 minutes. And here I am; I got a wife and kids waiting for me at home. I was just enamored with this process. I thought it was the greatest thing ever, because these people loved me.

Then I had this other dude. He found us through Google search when one of our videos popped up in the results. He was moving in for a job and said that everybody told him to look at the west side of Portland. This was a single dude in his 40s and was looking into Beaverton, Tualatin, and Tigard. We toured all those areas all day long. This was the first time that I actually listened to what a client really wanted from their space. So I asked him, "What do you really like doing? What's your favorite thing?" and he said, "I love riding my bike and hiking and running and jogging. I usually do 10 miles a day after work. I like hills, challenging stuff." That was when I knew for sure that these suburban areas out west were not for him. We go check out a spot called Multnomah Village. It's closer to downtown Portland, and it's super hilly with giant old-growth trees. It's right by Tryon Creek State National Park, which has 26 miles of all these just incredible trails through the trees with wooden bridges and all that. So it's all right there. When we drove in and he saw all the hills, windy roads, and people on bikes, I could see that it was much more his speed. We parked and took a hike down one of the trails. Then he turns to me and says, "Holy shit. This is the pinnacle. This is the dream. This is everything that I love." I'm thinking, '*hell* ye-ah, I'm getting this shit. I'm the maaann.' Come to find out,

3-4 months later, that he went into a new construction and got scooped up by the sales agents. This was the first time Jesse ever said he was going to send a glitter bomb to one of our clients. Jesse was all about these glitter bombs, and he hates new construction sales reps and builders. Don't even get him started on it unless you want to hear him get incredibly pissed because of just how shifty they are.

Then we get another couple, they were living here in Houston. They were moving to Portland because they could work from anywhere. They had a budget of $900,000 to a million bucks. I just about shit myself when I heard that. I was already calculating... Right, this is, like, $25,000! Oh my God. I do call after call with them. They can't make it into town yet, so I go and do all these video tours of these giant houses all over Portland. They sent me everywhere, and I was so happy. Then all of a sudden, a month or two goes by, and I never hear from them. They're gone. I'm like, "Hey, man, what's happened?" I kept messaging, messaging, messaging. "Yeah, we decided not to move there," they finally said. Frustrated as all hell, I say "Well, that's awesome. You could have told me that a while ago."

Then I had a New York guy. He had a $1.2 million budget. Drove him all over the city, looking at these super baller properties. Now, you guys know as real estate agents, you got to set up all these tours. It stresses me out. Honest to God, setting up property tours is the most stressful thing for me. If I saw a car in the driveway, I'd freak out because somebody could be home and I didn't know what to do. I don't know how you guys do it. So, I'm looking at $1.2M plus $900,000 (because I didn't know yet that the couple bailed hard) and there was another $800,000 in the pipeline. I'm telling Jesse we got 5 mill in the bank right now. This shit is getting real. I toured that dude all day long. Showed million-dollar properties in Northwest Portland. Sick as hell. Never heard back from him and Jesse found out later that he got hit by a car on his bike and decided not to move to Portland.

Had a guy reach out to me while I was touring another client, an older couple. They were looking at Vancouver, Washington. As I'm pulling up to pick up this couple, this guy calls, "Hey, Jackson. This really Jackson?" "Yes." At this time I was used to it, especially if it was a California number; I already knew it was a YouTube lead. "Alright, well, I got a budget of about... oh it don't really matter; 5, 7, 8 million, whatever I like." Holy shit. So I pull up to pick up these clients and they're like, "Oh my God, it's Jackson." They're waving at me while I'm in the car. But this guy was a little more important right about then. 5 *million* dollar client.

I'll get into that story in a little bit. But I toured these people all over Vancouver. I'm not licensed in Washington. Don't put me in jail. Toured them all day up in Vancouver. All freaking day. Dropped them off, talked to him a month later, and... "Sorry, we're not moving." I didn't know what was going on, but it wasn't going the way I thought it would.

Believe me when I tell you that I understand frustrations of new agents doing YouTube, when the calls start coming in but the closings don't. You'd be lucky to close anything in the first three months, it's more than six to nine. Look at this video thing as a month of content before you see results. In that time, you're going to do this and not get paid but after that, it's a gold mine. It goes a lot quicker than that for some people.

One day, Jesse calls and says to me, "Jackson, what's going on, man? None of these people are closing. What are you doing on the tours?" In my defense, I say " I'm taking them everywhere, and I'm going all freaking day. I'm wasting all this gas money." He comes back with his business brain, "Well, you need to set your priorities straight. Just tell them they get 2 hours." I'm like, "I can't, dude, they need these tours. They want to go see everything." Direct as always, he says "I don't give a shit. That's your time. That's your money. People will respect it and if they don't, tell them to go pound sand." That's Jesse for ya.

So on the next call, I told the people that we had 2 hours. And guess who it was? The Canadian couple. They were finally coming into town. "Hey, we got 2 hours blocked out. We're going to go show you these four houses, and after that, we can let you know some areas to go to." "Perfect. Thank you so much for your time. I can't believe you're actually giving us 2 hours." I'm over here thinking *Oh, my God, Jesse. I hate you. Why are you always right?* Jesse also said, "Hey, I'm going on this tour, and we're also going to charge these people

$500." I couldn't believe it, "Absolutely not. They're all going to hate us." Steadfast, he says "No, we're not going to charge them, but if they don't use us, we're taking the $500. If they use us to buy their house, we'll just give them a check, rip up the check or refund them at closing. But these people need to understand this is a business." So the Canadians came in. They wrote us a $500 check. We toured them, and they couldn't buy then. They didn't have American credit and it takes a while to build. In fact, you wanna know how long? They, being my first call ever, actually just closed about three months ago and Jesse still had their check. So that's how long this pipeline can be, but their tour set the bar for what was about to happen next.

Jesse said, "Alright, something is not working, and I'm going to start going on these tours with you, and I want to see what's happening." So Jesse would go on these tours, and he started asking the right questions to these people to get to know them. He'd check if they were preapproved. He's a damn good agent. He's also always looking for ways to streamline the process. So he decided that we needed to talk with these people beforehand on a Zoom call. When I heard that, I wasn't having any part in it. Nobody knew what Zoom was. At the time of writing this book, Zoom is the most recognized video conferencing platform because of Covid. But before Covid, it was foreign to many people. We'd get a lot of clients asking what Zoom was. But it was actually pretty easy to get them going on it. We'd send them the link, they'd download it, and it meant that we got to meet face to face.

That's when we started really noticing that people thought we were some kind of celebrities. Jesse and I loved it. That feeling of them seeing us and going, "Oh, my God, it's actually you." It's the craziest feeling in the world. Not only that, but we were Zooming before Zooming was a thing, and we could get all of those questions in to find the perfect spot for them. It allowed us to pull up the map and showcase areas, which would bring up more questions from them. Now we were able to start figuring out areas to take them to so that we weren't habitually wasting 2 hours at a time. It was the most efficient system, namely because we didn't have to pick them up, cruise around, and let them feel shit out. We were zeroing in on areas before seeing them in person. We were getting all that accomplished.

The one thing we realized right out of the gate that even though we were doing this initial Zoom call, these people needed to be preapproved. They needed lending options and we thought they'd got their own lenders. A lot of the time, that wasn't the case. We started helping people with the lending aspect. We also repeatedly stressed how important it was to have a local lender. That's when we started talking with Addy Nett. He's still our team lender to this day. 100% of his business is YouTube–that's how much he enjoys working with YouTube clients. Addy and I also started shooting videos together. We really hit it off, and we were editing videos together, and he was just killer. So we started leveraging him as our lender for these YouTube leads.

When we would try and relay information over to Addy, he had a lot of lender questions. It occurred to us that it was causing a major gap in the process, and it always required a second follow-up call, so it was creating more work. So Jesse asked him, "Hey, will you start attending all of these Zoom calls? Because 90% of the questions that these people have pertains to their budget, and they don't quite understand what their budget is." With that, Addy says, "Hell, yeah, man, I'll do it." So we started doing Zoom calls with Addy, and that became the new system. Cool as a cucumber, he would chill in the background. He would open up with something like, "Look, I'm just a part of their team. I'm the local lender here. Even if you have a lender already, that's fine. I am part of their team and just here to help." He's great at making people feel at ease, even with the most personal questions: "Perfect. Okay. Do you mind me asking about how much you think you'll be making?" "Okay, you got two vehicles." By the time the call was done, he would know just about everything he needed to know to assess the situation. He'd often realize that they had more budget to play with than they thought. Not trying to gouge anyone, always just trying to help them have a little more wiggle room.

Once we'd discussed it all with the client and knew their budget, Jesse would be able to figure out which areas were within reach. People would be set on an area that they couldn't afford, but Jesse could tell them about almost identical neighborhoods that they could buy in. Or, if they could now afford more, he was able to show them areas that they would never have even thought about before. It just completely redirected the conversations for the better.

The best part was that a lot of these clients were from YouTube. They were from all over. Instead of relocating within Portland, many of them were moving into Portland. That meant that they might be three, six, or nine months out. That gave Addy time to work his magic. He started saying to people in the Zoom calls, “Hey, at the end of this call, I’m going to send you guys an email. I’ve got your emails from Jackson and Jesse. What I’m going to do is just follow up. We won’t pull credit, but now I can start having those private conversations with you about your finances and everything so that when you guys are ready, we can pull that trigger.” This led to a lot of very happy customers.

Back then we didn’t understand this, but take a moment to think about the psychology behind moving. Moving or relocating is one of the most difficult things on planet Earth. It can be scary. When you have people that you can lean on and you already know because you’ve seen them in videos and talked to them over video call, it makes moving so much less stressful. If you’ve ever been on vacation with your spouse and you’re both hangry as hell, trying to decide what restaurant, imagine trying to move. It’s so much, not to mention that you’re going all day, you both may legitimately be hangry–on top of everything else. It’s a step from vacay. I’ve moved a few times. It’s miserable. If you rely on someone to just get the questions out there and find the areas that fit you, that is the best feeling in the world. And now you have this local lender who says, "Hey, if you call me, I will be on the phone. Days, nights, weekends, I've got you." It's so much better.

Now they have an entire relocation team on their side. They're feeling amazing, and when we actually do close that deal, we're also helping them with contractors and everything. It takes the stress off. It's easing some pretty major pain points for them. And that's all without cold calling, working with people who actually want to work with you, and not having to drive around everywhere trying to guess what they want. We're also starting to recognize that YouTube clients sell closer to two years on average, as opposed to seven. That's because many of them are moving into the city and have had more time to explore and find something they like even better. These people don't know anybody else, and want to work with us again. We have kicked so much ass with this system. Well, not I, we–I can't close shit, but our team can and that team has grown quite a bit since then.

At the time, I kept getting all the phone calls, all of them, and I'm awful at follow-up. Jesse calls me one day and says, "Jackson, what's going on? You keep telling me you're getting all these calls. You keep talking about all these leads, but nothing's happening. You ain't closing shit." That's just how he talks. He's direct. And I was like, "You hurt my feelings." He goes on to say, "Are you following up? What's the system here?" It drove him nuts: "I want you to hand over every single name, number, whatever you have on every one of these leads." Well, it was all on sticky notes, and to this day, if you look in my phone, because I had my original cell phone number in my early videos, like an idiot. That's why I teach to put a general number in there because you can never scale and grow. I've had four agents partner with us who we've had to help step out of production because they get so many leads, and they all told me, "God, I should listen to you." They then got a general number. I've had this number for 15 years, and I had to get rid of it. It's the Team's now.

I gave Jesse all my sticky notes, all my names, and all my numbers. The numbers I had in my phone were from people calling me, because, like an idiot, I'd put my actual phone number on our OG vids. More on that in a second, but these names were like 'John Stuart YouTube,' 'Martin Smith YouTube,' 'Jennifer Lisa YouTube,' and that's how I just put them in my phone, hoping they'd call back. There was zero organization, but that's one thing about operating on the side of the brain that I do. Jesse is business, I'm video. And it showed when I handed over my mountain of notes and he had twelve of them in contract within a month or two. Oh boy, my systems were broken. That's what led to Jesse setting up Zoom, and that's what led to getting Addy on there. Us working together and all using our strengths but not weaknesses is what led to 450+ home sales.

After all that, Jesse called me, he says, "Jackson, you're never going to do real estate another day in your life. Just focus on videos. That is your only job." He was saying it in the way of, like, yeah, you're never doing real estate again because you suck so hard at it. I took it as, thank God, I'd never have to do it. It was the best day of my life. I went home, hugged my wife, and realized that I never had to cold call, go door to door, do open houses and tours… none of that stressful shit. All I need to do is what I love. "I'm going all-in," I said to my wife, and all-in I went. That's when the expansion started.

CHAPTER 13

Expansion & Starting the YouTube Agents

Expansion and the start of the YouTube Agents. For all you OGs out there, you'll remember when we were the YouTube Agents and not the Channel Junkies. Well, we tried trademarking our original name. Google didn't like it, and they slapped our wrists. Little did we know, YT with a play button is part of the YouTube trademark.

In order to talk about the expansion, it helps to look back chronologically. I'm actually looking at our Portland, Oregon channel right now, and I'm going to build you out a timeline. In some of the marketing courses people take for real estate or the books we read, or the speakers we listen to, you're not getting the full experience. Honestly, some of the people that have come through our training had immediate success and now sell their own YouTube courses. Thing is, they don't have the pain or the backstory of repeatedly getting their asses kicked. So I want to give you more of a timeline of how everything evolved to where it is today.

I've shot videos in Seattle, Washington, all the way to the Florida Keys, and everywhere in between. You cannot get farther than those two markets. In short, I get around. But I'd love to paint a picture to illustrate to you just how quickly this machine was moving.

Once I was freed up, we grabbed a new gear and got going. If I have a path or not, my mentality is to just go and not stop. When I was in high school, a top basketball player in the state, I had a coach come to me and say, "Jackson, you play for me, son, but you ain't going to start. In fact, you're red shirtin' in yer first year." I'm like, "red shirt? What the hell? Okay." But I signed and went to this local college. We started scrimmaging, playing, and the coach told me again, "You're red shirtin." It means that you sit out for an entire year but you don't lose a year of eligibility. What I found out is that by giving local kids scholarships, it opened the college up to get more scholarships to get kids from other major cities like Ohio, California, and all over. I was a great player, but now I'm playing with a bunch of great players. We started scrimmaging, and my mindset was that I was just going to just *kill* these dudes. I was going to work harder. I was going to go after it. Now, before the season even started, just from the scrimmages, that coach came out to talk to me. He was from Tennessee, had the strongest Southern accent. The boys and I love joking about it now. He said, "Jackson, oh boy. Well, you ain't red shirtin' and son, and in fact, you're startin'." Hell. Yes.

Later, when I was told to get my Master's because that's how I could move up from a lineman to a manager, I completed it in 5 months. I went to Texas to do my lineman apprenticeship. It's a three-year apprenticeship. I did it in two years and one day. So I've always gotten stuff done really, really fast. And now that I was freed up to do video for our channels, expansion was happening really, really fast.

But there was a lot of pain. I'll talk more about this in the next chapter; the time I was probably the most depressed I've ever been and it was due to the work I put in and not seeing any results at all. I wasn't able to provide for my family the way I wanted, I wasn't closing, and shit was not working. The time that I quit, all of it. It was so brutal that I almost didn't look back. But more on that later.

As I look at our Portland, Oregon channel, I'm looking at where our YouTube started in 2018. I had just got my real estate license in August or September of 2018. I was all-in on cold calling, door-knocking, and all that stuff. January 2019 was when we were going heavy on the Digital Mayor Now play. There are Digital Mayor Now teaser videos, podcasts, a day in the life of a real estate agent. So January was when we really started digging into YouTube. We then did a 'Living in Sellwood, Portland' vid. Many people wouldn't have even heard about Sellwood. It's a really popular area that the locals know well. Then I remember Jesse telling me, "Hey, we need to show the top neighborhoods of Portland, like Alberta Arts District."

So there's an Alberta Arts District full vlog tour. Then we went and did the Pearl District. Our plan was to show off the best areas. What I learned was that, just like many of the people reading this, most people have probably never heard of Sellwood, Alberta Arts, or the Pearl District. Why would you have, unless you're from or live in Portland? So those videos never really took off.

So we moved to covering shops, restaurants, bars, and doing interviews. This is going through all of February. I mean, every day, I've got videos going to YouTube, but all of these videos were made for Instagram or Facebook. If you click on them, there's a square with a big black bar on the top and bottom with big white Impact font letters. They weren't getting a ton of traction either. So, on February 25 of 2019, I shot a pros and cons video:

What's up, everybody? This video is going to be about five things that I love about Portland and five things I hate about Portland. So stay tuned.

As of May 12th, 2023, so just over four years after it was published, that video has 58,184 views and 674,395 impressions. You look at that video and we crushed it. But I will never forget my opinion of that video when I shot it, thinking "this shit does not work." I remember it had three views, nine views, then it had probably 20 views. I was sharing it to a real estate Facebook group at this point. When I originally posted the pros and cons to YouTube and Facebook on February 25, it went nowhere. Fell flat on his face. It had the worst thumbnail and didn't have the description built out. Now you go and look at this, and it's got a killer thumbnail. You can always change things. For that video, I've probably changed the thumbnail 20 times, split testing.

The next video is dated February 27. It was a 'Sushi Bazooka – How to Make California Rolls.' What the hell was I thinking?! I mean, it's a killer video, though. It's really funny, too. But what on earth does it have to do with real estate? March 3rd, Shoals Heights elementary. That's when we got called up because we were doing so much local stuff already. Then on March 5th, I do a *Cost of Living in Portland, Oregon* video. That came about because I had started doing keyword research. It was something getting searched a good amount. Today, the *Cost of Living in Portland, Oregon* vid has 33,961 views. Both of those videos were shot on cell phone.

March 13th we run an advertisement for a listing in Portland, on how to sell your house. It went a little something like this:

Alright, so you live on the west side of Portland. You're thinking of selling your home, but you don't want to pay those outrageous prices to list your house. Well, then, I have the exact plan you need.

A 1% listing, just like the big names, but I do ten times more. You're going to have the most beautiful professional photos, a community and a property video, and I'll build you a custom website for your property, and I'm going to get it out to 800+ syndicated sites. It will be everywhere. It's going to be marketed better than any 6% listing out there, and I'm doing it for less. We are selling homes fast and for top dollar.

Hi, my name is Jackson Wilkey with Next Home Realty Connection, and I created this special program just for you. So make sure you tap that link to learn more information. I really want to help you save a ton of money and sell your home fast.

Man, this is getting painful listening to this. Is that the most salesy shit you've ever read? When nothing's working, you'll try anything. Running ads was life back then; you gotta get eyeballs on these videos. But, good night–that literally makes my skin crawl. 9,681 views and you might be like, damn, that's cool. Every one of those views was paid for. I got 10,000 views on that and no calls.

A lot of agents were doing property tours and listing videos, so Jesse was busy. He had a lot of listings. Then on April 4, 2019, we did the *Top 5 Neighborhoods in Portland, Oregon*. That was where I really started to experiment with vlogging. I was tired of doing all that other shit. It wasn't working. What are the videos that people are looking for? They want to know both sides of a place. So I did *Top 5 Neighborhoods* as well as *Top 10 Worst Areas to Live in Portland, Oregon*. The latter is a pretty rough vlog. It's a fun one, but I remember it was a drizzly day. I shot it with my phone, and it's kinda blurry. Look today and it's got 30,000 views.

Then, a listing video shot by Jesse:

Hey, what's going on? This is Jesse Dau with the Real Agent Now Group, and I am here because you are thinking about selling your house for sale by the owner. I

I'm going to give you five amazing tips on how to get your house sold by yourself. I'm also going to give you some insights on what to expect when listing your house for sale by owner.

Hey, you might even have your house on the market, but you are just sick and tired of being inundated with phone calls from real estate agents.

I have created five amazing tips that I'm going to share with you. Also, down below in the comments section, there are the five links to my tips. There's the Home Prep guide. There are referrals for all these five great tips that I'm going to give you. A referral for escrow, and your Escrow agent is going to be able to give you all of your Oregon real estate forms to get your transaction completed. So without further ado, here are those five amazing tips that I'm referencing.

Hahahaha, oh boy. Doing these videos starting out was brutal. On that one, if you watch it, Mr. J Dau's eyes are wide open and off to the side. He's reading a script. It's just what we did. We were salesy and trying to be people we weren't. That's just some funny shit right there.

It got to April 11th, 2019, and I've been licensed now since August 2018. Yep, I did not get my first deal until April 2019. In fact, I've only ever closed two deals. Kinda notorious for that. But I was broke and starving and would do anything. Now, if you remember, I had that neighbor in the beginning who wanted me to sell his house for just 4%. Hell, yeah I did it, and I made the most killer listing video of all time.

On April 16, 2019, we did a video of Lake Oswego, Portland. That was the first vlog where we incorporated drone shots into the video. We had been doing a lot of drone at this point for the listing videos, but this is the first time we did it for vlogging. When viewing it later during the editing process, I remember thinking 'this is next level - this is cool.' Here's a snippet of the audio:

Alright, so you want to know what it's like to live in the Lake Oswego, Oregon, area? So, this video is all about living in and what to do in Lake Oswego, Oregon. But there's one thing you've got to know. You won't believe it.

That hook "you won't believe it" hook at the end is to keep people on the video for longer. If you keep some of the valuable information for later in the video, you get longer view times. Longer view times means that your video will rank higher. It's all about view time.

At this time, we had been taught that shorter videos were better because "people have a short attention span." I can tell you now, that is bullshit. Particularly when people are playing the video in hopes of learning something new, something they want to know. Longer is better. Right where we were doing 2-minute-ish videos. Then we had a 17-and-a-half-minute video, which is kind of on the short end of what I do now. But back then, that was like the longest video on planet Earth, as far as real estate was concerned. So I cut it down. I now know that was a mistake, but you live and you learn.

Now we're starting the vlog and this is when the channel is taking off. For the next video, we headed out to Hillsboro. We'd been told by a reliable source that it was the next hottest market in Portland. So we did a video entitled *Best Suburbs to Live on the West Side in Portland, Oregon*. We shot 16 minutes, and I got my truck towed. In case I haven't said it enough, I was broke as a joke. I had parked at a Starbucks. I got back to my truck, and my truck was gone. It was $500 to get it out of the impound lot. I remember telling my wife that, and she just broke down crying. We had no money at all. That was an extremely painful day.

June 4, 2019, we shot *Where to Live in Portland, Oregon When Moving to Portland, Oregon*, at Tilikum Crossing. That was the day that I created the call to action. It's almost three years to the date I'm writing this. That's the day we started getting phone calls. We had been getting the attention from the vlogs but only a couple of reach-outs before we spoke to Addy's ex-boss–the bank owner who told us we needed to tell people to call, and we needed to do it right in the beginning of our videos. It felt amazing.

June 11, *Living in Vancouver Washington vs Portland*. Bingo. That's when I learned about traffic sources.

That is also when we started getting a ton of reach outs. You can see in the videos from about this point on where when we're shooting our intros with confidence, you'll see Jesse with his hands twirling in the air. When I say hit that subscribe button, he's poking at his phone. When I say call us, he's got it up to his ear. We're confident and we were cocky, and we loved it. The comments blew up. Agents loved us. This is when you can see we were going all-in.

Then we went and shot a video at Nike's world headquarters. The thumbnail had golden Jordans on it. This video started to take off and go viral, and then Nike called and basically said, 'kids, shut this video down.' They seemed to think we were profiting off of them. Usually, Jesse tells every person to just pound sand. Relocation companies, don't even try to mess with Jesse. He's keeping his money. But when Nike called, he said "take the video down." Same way, when we were the YouTube Agents and Google called, Jesse said, "we got to rebrand." He knows the uphill battles we can't win.

July 9, 2019 this is when we're going so hard. Three videos a week, but we couldn't keep doing the vlogs. I couldn't keep up. So we started doing what were called filler videos. Still, none of this real estate content is working. Jesse said we need to just shoot a video telling people to call. He's that direct. He's like, we're going to do a video about six things people need to know, and it's basically just going to be, "hey, call us and don't mess around." Later, this was a video that we saw a ton of agents start doing. Never gets the most views, but good Lord, you get a lot of calls from it.

So we did that, and this is when we started doing the filler videos. We did one called *How to Find a Perfect Investment Property in Portland.* Jesse knows a lot about cap rates and numbers. Now, I know these videos don't perform that well. They get the least amount of views. But man, they speak right to the heart of investors. And we picked up a couple with this vid. One of those investors has bought and sold 6 properties with us for around $5 million.

We're getting more and more and more confident. This is the end of July and early August. This is also when I closed the second deal of my career. I didn't really do much of it because Jesse did the majority of it. It was the first YouTube deal. I'll never forget we were touring the Canadian couple, and I got a Facebook message. I didn't believe it at first, thinking it was a scam or a shitty Zillow lead. This guy hits me up. He tells me that he's been watching all of our YouTube videos. He had found a house and needed our help to buy it. We've all seen this kind of message, and they're usually complete and utter shit. So I kind of just put it away. I told Jesse about the message and he figured we may as well hit this guy up. I did and he was a real dude. He was super weird. He was tattooed up, coming from California, riding a Harley Davidson. He and his wife were just some rugged people, man. They were looking in Gresham, Oregon, which is not a pretty place. He's like, "we're coming from a shithole in California where our manufactured home had recently been shot up. How bad can it be?" When I went and looked at this $200,000 house, it was bad. But we sold that thing, and that was the second closing I'd ever had. He only lived there for a year and called us back to sell it! I guess Portland was worse than LA in his mind.

We're a year into this now. After twelve months of pain, agony; thousands of videos, podcasts, different marketing companies, and Facebook groups, I wanted to get this message out there to other agents. Like, this is how you truly do it and truly get phone calls. So we did and we named it *The YouTube Agents.*

Not long after that, something magical happened. For the first six months of being licensed, I lived and died by one podcast. Joshua Smith GSD Mode. I would listen to him everywhere I went. I love this guy's podcast. So, we had just started the YouTube Agents. One day, I get a call, but it's not from a real estate client. It's from Joshua Smith. He's like, "What's up, bro? Dude, your YouTube channel's fucking crazy. I've never seen anything like that. I've literally been watching all the videos." I'm freaking out. He's like, "I got to get you on our podcast." That was an absolute dream. It was crazy. He then called us back almost twelve months to the date to come on for a second time, and here's what he had to say:

This time I wanted to bring them back on the podcast. Now that it's been a year later, and you guys, the growth that they have experienced from YouTube videos, now these are free mediums. Obviously, YouTube is free for all of us. We can all go out there and grow our YouTube presence, our YouTube channel, and our real estate business.

Whether you're a real estate agent looking to go out there and gain buyers and sellers from your YouTube channel, or you are a team leader or broker-owner that's looking to go out and recruit agents from your channel, this is such a highly effective medium and a highly effective tool, and you're going to see from our guests today, you guys have totally changed every dynamic of your lives. They've been able to both relocate out of the state and run their team virtually as well as it's allowed them to expand to eight different markets with their expansion team.

Now just one of their channels, their original channel up in Portland, Oregon, year to date, they've already done 25 million in gross volume sales just from their YouTube channel alone and just that one location. They are now up to 50+ leads each and every day from their YouTube channels, and these are high-quality leads. These are as high quality as a referral. These are people that know them, like them, and trust them to the connection they built through their YouTube channel.

Now, before the first interview that we did with Joshua Smith, he also reached out to ask if we had anything we wanted him to promote. "Courses, anything like that, just let me know. I'll be more than happy to do it." The coolest thing about Josh Smith is he just puts everybody up. He's always helping people. I've always remembered that. But I didn't have a course at the time, and we had just launched the YouTube Agents. But Jesse's got that business mind, don't you forget that. I don't remember exactly the date, but it was pretty quick. Jesse came to me and said, "Jackson, you've got to build a course, dude." I'm like, "Hell, no."

Again, my mindset, I can't close. I don't like to be salesy. I hate being hated, and I'm like, if I build this course, everybody's going to think I'm salesy. All the while, he's reminding me that we're doing this to help people. Since that date to now, we've sold over one thousand courses. Jesse called me not too long ago and said, "Do you realize that 95% of our students do not finish 10% of your course?" That was crazy to me. I had made it so easy and gone through so much pain. I built this 'copy & paste' course from A to Z, and the people that did it and followed it are the ones closing 100 homes a year. Yet 95% of people don't complete 10% of it. That was nuts to me.

Guys, I cannot stress this enough. We have paved this road to where you do the right videos, have the right keywords, the right thumbnails and descriptions, shoot the proper content, have the right calls to action, the right hooks, and you will get the business. You may only be getting 30 views, 90 views out of the first few weeks. Maybe you're stuck at 300 subscribers. Or maybe you only got one call this week, but it is worth it. I promise you that. I showed the shorter timeline to reiterate the amount of effort that went into this. So, yes, I love that we've made this super easy, but you have to realize that there was a crazy amount of effort behind it, and there were so many trials and tribulations.

So we built that first course. But then we started talking about expansion. We were killing it in Portland, and Seattle is only 3 hours away. Jesse was licensed in Washington. The median home price in the area of Seattle we were looking at was somewhere around $900,000. So, everything we sold would be coming in around a million bucks. We could set it up just like the Portland channel. So on November 9, 2019, we drove up to Seattle and spent a day there. We ended up shooting four different vlogs and capturing a ton of b-roll all over Seattle. We went to Pike Street, the famous open-air fish market where they throw fish across from one stall to the next, and that's where we got our intro:

What's up, everybody? Welcome to our YouTube channel, Living in Seattle, Washington, where our goal is to show you everything about eating, working, sleeping, playing, and living here in Seattle, Washington. So if you are new to this channel, make sure you subscribe, and you click that little bell. So you're notified every time we do a new video.

We're local real estate agents that have an absolute passion for helping people move to the Seattle market. We know how difficult it is when you're looking online, watching videos, and trying to find that perfect home for you and your family. That's right. It is incredibly difficult to find the perfect location. That's our job for you.

I remember watching this video of these guys at a YouTube conference, and I get this question every day from agents, and so I was trying to figure it out too. The question is *how many videos should you be posting on your YouTube channel?* One of the guys on this video said, "You do not want to post videos every other day or every day because what you're doing is you're kind of fighting your video with the algorithm. So YouTube's only going to rank one of your videos right out of the gate in the first 24 hours. So if you do a second one, it may pull the first one out." I don't know if that's true or not. That's just what he said. He said the best recipe is every other day. So driving home, I said, "Jesse, I'm going to go do videos every other day for all three channels." Usually, Jesse says, "Fuck yeah, let's do it." Do you know what he said to me? "Are you sure? That's not going to be too much, and it's going to hurt production." I was sure.

At this point, I am in a rhythm. I absolutely loved the Portland channel because all the vlogs were starting to look really great. We're closing deals, and I have real self-worth for the first time in a long time. Now I'm teaching the YouTube Agents, and I'm helping agents do all this the correct way. I've always had a dream of being on a stage. I never knew for what. But I was also like, hey, I want to create a YouTube channel teaching everything that I know. So, getting to do that was like me speaking on a stage, getting to teach.

After getting back from Seattle, and I'm thinking, 'this is going to be no problem, Jesse. A video every other day.' Well, if you do the math, some weeks, that's four videos a week per channel. So that is twelve videos a week, to shoot, edit and post. On alternate weeks, it's nine videos a week–still a lot. So we did that. I shot a video every other day for every single one of these. On March 21, 2020, after 48 videos on the Seattle channel, I quit. You can go and look. March 21, 2020, was the last video you'll see with my face in it. It wasn't working up there. We got our asses kicked up there. I also started realizing I didn't really care about Seattle. So it was really hard for me to get videos out. I was basically just reading blogs at this time and kind of transcribing it into my words. I quit. That was a tough day. I'll never forget the depression that I was feeling at that point.

CHAPTER 14

Depression & All My Mistakes

I thought I would do a chapter on where I was mentally with all the Seattle stuff. As well as all of my mistakes. I'm usually such a glass-half-full guy, I got to have fun, I got to get through the hard stuff just because I want to be happy. But I'm going to talk about a shitload of mistakes that I've made, some that were really funny, and hopefully, it'll help you to avoid making those same damn mistakes.

The psychology that went behind where I was after those 48 videos in Seattle at the time is not explainable. I just mentioned I'm a glass-half-full guy. In fact, my glass is so damn full it's spewing over. I hate confrontation, I hate drama, I will laugh off anything, and I just always want to be happy and positive. So to have the weight of the world on my shoulders and the Seattle channel just not producing, I felt like I had to answer for that. I wanted to quit long before the 48 videos. You could probably watch some of those end ones and feel, 'Yeah, he is zapped of energy.' I felt like, *damn, I did it in the Portland thing. I figured it out. It's working there. We're getting reach-outs, and this is a more expensive market, it should be way better.* But it didn't work. Then I'm thinking that I was a total fraud, like Portland was a fluke. I mean, how can I go into one market, finally figure it out, crack this code, start teaching agents this stuff, go try and duplicate it, and it didn't work? Also, I was going to let Jesse down. That's been one of my biggest fears in business. A guy who's so direct, who tells you exactly the way things are going. I did fear the repercussions of telling him that something wasn't working. So I figured I'd just continue to work harder until it does. I thought he was going to hate me. I wasted all his time, energy, money And now the Seattle thing–it's all my fault.

I also started getting really short with my wife, and my kids. I had to get twelve videos a week shot, and I was editing all of them too. So I'm letting people down all over the shop. The craziest thing about my wife is she will literally do anything for anybody. She is the sweetest human I've ever met in my life, and I never knew how to go to her when I had a problem or to Jesse, my business partner. It's crazy. And I'm telling you, in this book, I'll just get to everything. I'm opening up because I just hope that it helps somebody else out there who's feeling some of the same things.

In the past month or two, since writing this book, I've started to have discussions with my parents. I'm now 37 years old, and I shot them both a video. I was frustrated and I couldn't write to them. I opened up and told them that I had this great childhood. My parents were so nice, but the affection was not there between them. I never saw them hug. We never went on vacations together. They were great, nice people, and I had a great childhood, but I also asked my wife, "Is there a way that you can have a great childhood but also a shitty one?" I was starting to wonder why I could not show my wife attention out in public. It feels very awkward for me. It always has been. Back when I was in middle school, my parents got a divorce, and I remember it being the best that had happened in my life up to that point. They finally were themselves, they were fun. For a long time, all the way through the time I was in middle school, they coexisted, thinking they were doing my sister and I a favor by living together and staying together. They did it for us. So they never showed each other attention. They never talked, and we never communicated. There just wasn't any of that growing up. I'm telling you, people who know my parents are like, "They're the nicest people ever. They're the coolest." I'm like, "Yeah, but it was a little weird in there." So I was never taught to open up to people. I never talked with my parents about all this until just recently.

Now here I am, running a business and I'm in deep. I'm from Idaho, where you work, you punch the clock, you go home and do it all over again. Entrepreneurship is not taught or highly regarded there and old ways of life are very prominent. That's what I had done my whole life. All of a sudden, I'm running this business and am letting down all these people–people I love and adore. I don't know how to communicate how I'm feeling. I just get shit done. I'm Jackson Wilkey, I tell people I'm getting my master's done in six months, they laugh in my face, and I do that shit in 5. So, I can't quit. I was in a really weird place.

The thing that aggravates me the most about not being able to get emotions out is that my kids are my life and I wasn't doing them any favors by bringing that to the table. So I've learned to communicate with them a million times better because I didn't have that right for the longest time. Now I open up about these things, I'm honest and I ask them to tell me the truth; let's have these conversations. It's been amazing, and I've learned a lot of that from running a business and getting my ass handed to me with these YouTube channels. Guys, literally, when I say I've coached thousands of agents, I've had thousands of calls with agents. You wouldn't believe where some people's minds are at. We think, oh, all I got to do is shoot a YouTube video. I don't know where your headspace is. I don't know what's going on at home. Maybe you got sick, parents got sick, whatever. When people are scared of the next step, about not knowing how to do something, we'll sometimes make excuses as well. But did you know that doing new things literally creates new neural pathways in your brain? So, even if you fail a thousand times, you're getting smarter for it.

Today I tell people, "Don't ever quit. Keep going. You got to keep putting in the work." I didn't have anybody to lean on back then to tell me to do that. Now there are thousands of agents doing this YouTube thing who can say, *Yeah, I remember getting my ass kicked for the first three, six months, but Jackson just said, keep going, and all of a sudden it started working.* But I quit, so how can I tell these people to keep going?

Well, it's not until now that I realize it's a pipeline business, and especially in more expensive markets like Seattle, it just takes longer. Back then I couldn't see the light at the end of the tunnel and felt like I'd been searching for it for too long. I was going to be letting Jesse and all these other real estate agents down. I was depressed, spiraling out of control. I got to a point where I could not physically shoot another video. I was so mentally drained and I could not think. Even for the YouTube Agents for Portland, I just was physically and mentally done. I went to Jesse, and I can't remember exactly if he asked me what's up with the Seattle channel or if I just went to him, but I said, "Dude, it's not working, and the only select few calls that we got are just renters." And he's like, "Alright, well, cool. What are you going to do?" I'm like, "I don't want to focus on it anymore because it's just ruining me." I'm at this majorly depressed stage, and it's hard for me to open up like that. I was expecting wrath from him. But that fucking guy has got life figured out. He goes, "Perfect. Drop it. Fuck it, if it doesn't work, let's just stop." Taken back, I say "What, that's it?" He responds, as calm as can be, "Yeah, dude. I mean, we're not going to waste our time. I don't waste time and money. If it doesn't work, it doesn't work. It's a more expensive market. We were both thinking that it's double the price, so we're going to make double the money. But it's not working."

This is why when people take our courses and have this instant success. I got my ass kicked and can teach by stories. I know that in these expensive markets, it just takes a little bit more time. I know the way you have to speak.

I'd been beyond stressed and Jesse made it ok. I read one time that Trader Joe's, one of my favorite stores, every single year, they look at their sales. They take the top 20% of producing products. They keep those. The bottom 80%, they get rid of and they bring in 80% new inventory. They only keep the top 20%. That's how Jesse's mind works. I was putting in the effort, he knew that. So, he said "Screw it, quit it." So I did, and that felt amazing.

I kind of got my groove back, and was able to refocus on the Portland thing, which was paying. I went all-in on the YouTube Agents. That was kind of my new baby, as well as the *Living in Portland, Oregon*, channel. We put Seattle on hold. I'll talk later about what happened to that channel and its success. It's been one wild ride. Nowadays, I can give you examples of every single kind of market you could start a channel for because I've done them all. From the largest cities to the smallest digs in the country, from ocean views to mountain towns, to deserts; I've done them all. During which, I got my ass kicked with communication. That has been one of the hardest things for me in this journey. My advice for you is to surround yourself with people that you can have these conversations with, who can lift you up, who can just say, "Yeah, you're good. That's fine. Don't focus on that shit."

Giving up on the Seattle channel when I did was one of the best things that could've happened. It's just like in real estate: hate cold calling and door knocking as I did, there's another way. I should have never spent 1 second doing it. If I'd have known what I know now, I would have been going hardcore on YouTube from the start. In the last chapter, I went through the timestamps with 12-14 months of no paydays. It was 6-7 months before I got my actual first deal. A dude who actually believed in me enough to give me 20% of his business, a friend who gave me 20 grand that I blew on dumbass websites that I don't even use anymore. Through all that, I'd say that the key is opening up and being honest with the people around you. You got to talk about this stuff, because if you don't, your business and relationships will fail.

How can you have a book about YouTube, and then here I am crying and talking about feelings? Because I know after all this and thousands of coaching calls, that 99.99999% of it is mental. That's what I help people get over. It's not this magic, "Yeah, do this video title, and it will work." No, there's a little psychology behind the videos. It's all about understanding exactly who you are and getting your niche and your stories out there. That's what I've helped people do more than the logistical stuff.

You may have heard before that if you look at the five people you surround yourself with, and I'll tell you who you're going to be. So that's why we continue to surround ourselves with absolute ballers, both male and female. I also think that getting a partner is super helpful, somebody who is 180° out from you, so that you can keep each other in check. I'm sure I'm going to force Jesse to get his story out one day, and he's probably going to have some shit that I've never heard before. He's had some dark times to where he's been able to just pick up that phone and call me. 99% of our calls are just us catching up. He knows everything about me, my kids, my passions, and he also knows you don't step on those boundaries. It's really cool to have that.

So, the mistakes: When I shot videos at first, I was very hard on myself, and I edited, edited, edited. Then I got to a point where I was shooting so many I didn't care anymore. So there were massive mistakes like audio missing; for that I would do a quick voiceover. I just got the videos out because I was dead set on getting enough content out there. When it came to using a green screen, I took two nails in my framing hammer, I took my son's blanket, flipped it back because it was green, put it against the wall and hung it. It had all the stitching lines in it but I didn't care. I didn't want to wait one day to get my green screen. I wanted to get those videos out now, and that's what I did. So I used this baby blanket and it actually worked, believe it or not. But I had no idea about lighting, the distance to the camera. I was only just learning to edit.

I finally get this portable green screen. Well, I start shooting videos, and there's this really fuzzy line around me. It's because I had no idea about lighting and distance away from the green screen. I found out that there has to be really good lighting, and if you're in ambient light and it's not controlled, it'll get fuzzy. I realized that at the very least, I needed to get a ring light. That's what everybody was using, these 18-inch ring lights. Then you put your phone right in the middle of your light and then use the green screen. I would get the room really dark and use that light, and I started getting a much clearer picture. I liked it, but it still was fuzzy. That's when I learned that when you stand with your back up against a green screen, the light that's hitting you is then reflecting onto the green screen. If you're standing really close to it, you'll have a very dark green shadow that's about a half inch to an inch right around your head. It's a different shade of green, so when you try to clean that out, the computer doesn't know the difference, and it makes this fuzzy line. I started standing farther away from the green screen, like 1-2 feet. Now, when the light would hit me in the face, it would cast my shadow out really wide, like a foot or two, and it was very faint. That led to those crispy ass lines I'd been looking for. After figuring that out, my green screen game rose to 100%.

Then one day, I shoot this video and go to edit it. If you've ever done green screen, what you do is you take the video file, and then whatever your green screen background is, you stack that on top. You then hit the key element, and what it does is it erases the green screen. But this time when I did that, my whole fucking body was erased. There was just a head sitting there. I was wearing a green golf shirt, and since it was green, it erased. I was like, 'I don't care. I'm releasing it.' So there's a video out there somewhere with just my head talking. Really brings a fresh meaning to Talking Head style video. So, make sure you don't wear green or blue shirts.

Next up: microphone issues. I recorded two chapters of this book two days ago, and my microphone was unplugged. There is nothing more debilitating and frustrating than shooting a video, or in my case, a 35-minute segment of a book and the damn microphone wasn't on. I've done this a few times. Early on, the GoPro would be a little bit glitchy, or it would unplug, or something would happen, and we would shoot these videos, but there was no sound. Yes, I've done an entire day of Vlogging, and later realize that there's no sound. Brutal.

I learned with my GoPro to click record, and talk into it, "test, test, test, test, video," or whatever. Or something like "Now, brown cow the Human Torch was denied a bank loan." Anchorman, for those who didn't know. Then I'll turn the camera off and replay it just to make sure I can hear the recorded sound.

I recently shot four videos. Two for Houston, two for Portland. I'm always four weeks ahead, so all I've got to do is shoot one video a week and a missed week here or there doesn't matter because I have four weeks of backup ready to go. So I shot four videos and recorded two chapters of this book, and the damn microphone was not plugged in, so it sounded like I was 40 ft away, talking in a hollow room.

One time I was in Nashville for two straight days. 20 videos in two days. I looked at our entire intro for Living in Nashville and the video froze. That's when my GoPro Hero 7, our very first camera finally shit out on me and froze up. So we haul ass back to downtown to shoot the Living in Nashville intro again before hauling ass back to the airport. It also took us about four tries because the GoPro kept freezing up. It finally had enough. To be fair, it'd shot like a thousand videos. It was worth its weight in gold and maybe more.

Jesse, this is his story, but I'm a better storyteller, so I'll tell it. He had the drone. I never flew a drone a day in my life, and people ask me about drones all the time. I didn't do it. That was Jesse. This dude. We would pull up into these dark alleys. It was early on when drones were just starting to come out, so there weren't a ton of regulations yet. Now they can straight-up shut your drone down for flying in the wrong area. So we would pull into these dark alleys in Portland. He has a sunroof and would just stick his hand up out of the sunroof, put the drone on the roof, and fly that son of a bitch all through Portland, buzzing through these buildings. He would fly him through these steel bridges. He was a renegade. Jesse also lived in the Pearl District, and he was way up on the 14th floor. He had one of the most iconic views. So he launched his drone from his room to get all this b-roll. In general, we had the sickest b-roll drone footage ever. We could get all the downtown and all the bridges. That thing flew for miles, and it worked. One day, he has launched this thing out of his place. He got it almost all the way back, when it started beeping and going ape shit. He's calling me and freaking out, "Oh my God, this drone won't come back. I don't know what to do." What happened was it sensed the building and so it wouldn't come back into his room. He kept trying to fly it down but it wouldn't go. He ends up finally going up really high and flying it down as fast as he can till it beeps, beeps, beeps, and comes to a screeching halt. Then he grabs it as its trying to fly away and it's like a game of tug of war. It worked. Dude, the things he did with that drone are unbelievable and our footage is insane.

One time I had to get a bunch of videos out. Unfortunately, I had a little spot on my cheek, that I had to get that removed. It had become cancerous. So they dug this giant ass hole out of my face and then stitched it up. I looked like Freddy Krueger. I had 20 stitches from the bottom of my eye all the way into the middle of my chin. But I had to shoot a video. So you know me, I like to get up close. I had this giant cut and all these stitches in with puss hanging out of them. I didn't care, I shot it anyway. You know what's crazy about that video? I got so many comments from people saying, 'Oh, that's mole surgery,' 'I had it. My dad had it. My uncle had it.' People sent their best wishes in the comments of that video, saying that they were glad I found it and got it taken care of. Nobody cared about the way it looked. So, if I can shoot videos with a swimming pool-sized hole in my face, you guys can too. But now we're going to get into that third channel. It's going to get good.

CHAPTER 15

Let's Try This Again... Oh, and F The Haters

On March 21st, 2020, after 48 videos in Seattle, I pulled the plug on that bitch. On May 12th, 2020, so just a couple months later that's the day I launched my first video in North Idaho. So how did this channel come about? As you know from this book, that's where I'm born and raised. In the last 20-25 years, Idaho has been a relocation mecca.

Now Jesse, and maybe you're this type of person or you know somebody like this, but Jesse's the kind of person, if I really want to know an answer to something, whether it's good or bad, I'll just ask him because he's usually right. Sometimes it's scary. With Seattle, Jesse was the man. He said stop that shit. But he's never ever just good with, just working with what we got. I call him Mr. Revenue Streams because he's finding us so many different revenue streams. Well, I call him 'Three Forks', because of the multiple streams in Three Forks Montana.

Once I was free from the depression of Seattle, the creative juices started flowing again. Portland and the YouTube Agents were back on track. It was time for a new challenge. I was sitting there telling Jesse that North Idaho is only six hours away from Portland, it's quick to get to, I really wanted to start a channel there. I felt like I could be very relatable with North Idaho because I knew it through and through. I went up to Seattle, I got nothing, I don't even really like Seattle. And it kicked my ass. I know every square inch of North Idaho. Literally every square inch. I know every house, every street, every neighborhood. It's a small area. I can ride my four wheeler from my dad's house in Coeur d'Alene all the way to Montana via mountain back roads and never touch a main road. Jesse's response was this "Hell no. Nobody's moving to Idaho." I got where he was coming from, but realized that maybe he didn't know that it'd been a super sneaky relocation market for four to five decades. Now if you tell a local Idahoan that, they're so small minded that, nope, it's just today people are moving here. In all actuality, we saw the biggest boom at the end of the 90s into the early 2000s.

A little backstory: I was in high school in the early 2000s. I was also working full time at this ranch I grew up working on, so I'm a ranch hand. I loved it. In fact, I wanted to work there full time as a rancher. It was hard work, working with cattle, doing all that. But every day after work, we'd be drinking beers, and talking. The guy who owned the ranch was also a high-end builder, so I got to hear about all that. It was one of the best times of my life.

After high school I was going to go play college basketball. Right after graduation, I got a job down at the Coeur d'Alene Resort in Hagedon. This place sits on one of the prettiest lakes in the country, it's beautiful. The area was named Hagedon after Duane Hagedone, rest in peace to him. This guy made Coeur d'Alene, Idaho, what it is today. Yes it's a logging and mining town, but he had this big vision. So he built this freaking huge hotel downtown or maybe bought it and renovated it, I don't remember. For that, he was getting made fun of for decades, 'you're never gonna get people to this shithole town,' they'd say. You know what he did? He made it like one of the number one tourist attractions by getting the media involved. It really shone a light on the potential of North Idaho, and lots of people from around the country were seeing that. So, in 2002, USA Today ran a study. It turns out that we had the fastest growing economy in the entire country. We beat out Vegas, San Diego, everyone. This is back in the early 2000s when California was booming. All my friends, everybody wanted to move to California. My sister moved there. People were making tons of money in California, but we beat them. I'm reading this article, and realizing that I'm working for this ranch and that builder, and he is selling lots and building houses like crazy. Literally every swinging dick who could swing a hammer had a framing company and was building houses.

With all the new press and people seeing that stunning lake, Coeur d'Alene started to become popular with celebrities like Wayne Gretzky, Oprah,

Tiger Woods, John Travolta. They were flying in and buying these houses on the lake. When I was growing up, these cabins were like 80 grand, now they were selling for an average of 2.2 million. But the boom soon came to a halt when 2008 rolled around. It was devastating for North Idaho because there's no corporate structure there. So when the market crash of 2008 hit, there was not a job left in town. Everyone's businesses just crumbled up and died. All of my friends, we're all now in our mid-20s, every one of my friends went to North Dakota to go work the oil field or just got out of town. There was just zero work.

Before the crash it'd been a relocation hotbed because it's so frickin' pretty. And so when I was telling Jesse this. Now it's 2020, so the market's obviously back up and I knew people are starting to move to Idaho in droves and waves. This is just before Covid. And I'm saying to Jesse, "I'm telling you right now, you just don't understand. There are so many people moving to North Idaho." Framing companies, electricians, plumbers, you name it. People had started to build again. They're building million-dollar homes for all the California buyers. I thought it was a sure thing. Jesse responded with "I guess, you know, if you want to go waste your time, go do it."

The main reason I'm talking about all this is because, guys, when people ask me questions about YouTube, I've literally built a channel in the third largest city in the entire nation, Houston. I've also built YouTube channels where there were 11 homes for sale total because it's that small. So I really can understand where people are coming from, no matter where in the nation that is.

So, my wife, my kiddos and I packed up and drove to North Idaho. It took us seven days there. I needed to try it out and just see. It really dawned on me early on that without Jesse, I couldn't close shit, so I needed somebody I could trust in North Idaho who could close deals. So that was the first order of business.

I have a lot of really close personal friends in Coeur d'Alene. And I was thinking about taking that route at first, but I also was like, I know if this goes the way I'm thinking, it's going to be crazy. So I didn't want to give it to a friend who's going to be a slap dick and not close these things because it wasn't their idea to get a license. And I also don't want to just pick somebody who can do video because they could be just like me and if they were, they wouldn't be able to close.

It's crazy how the world works. I have this friend, Connor, that I kind of grew up with and became close with in university. He lived in the apartment below me and we became inseparable. We'd drink until 2 or 3 a.m. every morning, dollar Totino's pizza rolls at the ready. We just really hit it off in college. If we ever saw each other from there on out, we had a lot of funny sayings and inside jokes. It was a cool relationship. By the time I got back, he'd been in real estate for about three years. He put a post in Facebook, celebrating the year, it was like 41 million in sales volume in his third year. I also noticed that he'd been kinda posting a few podcasts and some videos. And obviously I knew those weren't really working for his business, but I was like, okay, he does some podcasting, he does videos, so he's not against it. And he did 41 million in sales, in a small town. So he must have systems in place to close deals. So I commented on his Facebook post, "Damn, homie, that's sick. Congrats! I may have a business proposition for you too." As it turned out, he had been thinking the same thing. So he was all-in.

We decided that I'd shoot all the videos and he would close them. As far as the money goes, it'd be a 50-50 split. I didn't want to touch any of his other business. Jesse and I would split each sale. So, Jesse would have 25% of. I'm going to do the work for this one, but this is our partnership. He gave me 20% of his business without thinking twice. It doesn't cross my mind, every single penny that comes in goes to both of us, and we cut it in half, right down the middle. It also wasn't like he wasn't doing anything. I told Connor that he'd also be working with Jesse on how we do our Zoom calls, schedule and business systems. The value for Connor was that I was going to come and build this damn thing, but him and his team closing it. People often ask how we pick partners and structures, at first we just had to kind of figure it out. A lot of it is about compatibility, but that they can do what Jesse or I can't.

So I go to North Idaho and we hit the road. We did all the vlogs and grabbed some killer b-roll. This is how I started creating my process; doing one major vlog and then vlogs of all the other cities around the main one. getting all the B-roll.

It was a beautiful day, so we went and golfed at the Coeur d'Alene Resort, where I worked right out of high school. There's a floating green there, so we get a bunch of B-roll of that. For this shoot day we hired a videographer, he was one of our friends. He followed us that day and took a bunch of shots. I had him for thumbnails and for B-roll. He's also a firefighter, but he does a bunch of real estate videography on the side. He grabbed drone footage and B-roll of all downtown Hayden and Coeur d'Alene. At the end of it, he said I could just have the folder. But I wanted to pay him at least something. So I ended up paying him like a couple hundred bucks and he sent me an entire folder of tons of b-roll. There were shots of summer functions, the carolines, downtown art on the green and a load more. It was just awesome. So I had all this sick-ass drone and r-roll footage. Connor and I started hitting the streets and vlogging. Then we went to his office, and shot a ton of videos.

We launched our first video May 12th of 2020. In 74 days, we had 1,000 subscribers. In our first 100 days, we had 1,400 subscribers and 70,000 views, and we'd closed almost 14 million in real estate. It was just million dollar buyer after million dollar buyer. It was *insane*. We were getting so many phone calls. I'm like, yeah, put that shit in your pipe and smoke it, Jesse.

Now this is also when I figured out that smaller markets are easier to rank quicker. So Portland, there was no other real estate agent doing this whereas Seattle is one of the most heavily vlogged cities. It took a lot longer to rank those videos, but it was also so expensive.

Becoming a true YouTuber, I'm starting to understand competition. Even if there are no real estate agents doing this in a particular market, you may have competition from other people who are using the keywords that you need to use. Certain markets you have the ability to go right in and dominate using the right keywords. For example, there were not a lot of videos for Coeur d'Alene, Idaho; Hayden Lake, Idaho; Post Falls, Idaho, or Rathdrum, Idaho. But when it came to Seattle, Washington, there were tons.

Right around the time that channel took off is really when I started getting hate for the first time. This is when I learned to not read comments. In Idaho, it's just behind the times. And with Covid and the mass relocation toward Idaho and Montana, housing went up 10x. That pissed people off no end.

Growing up there, it was this cool little quaint town. Even though it was getting busier while I was in high school, when I was a kid there were only two stoplights from my house in Hayden all the way to downtown Coeur d'Alene. Now there's like 20 of them, and the traffic's so atrocious. So locals get really disgruntled and they start blaming me. They tore my ass up. Even friends reached out to check in. It's a mining town. You can either work in the mine or you can sell the shovels to the miners. I always worked in the mine. Now, I was selling the shovels.

I will admit, however, that I did one of the dumbest fucking things ever. Now, the video had no intention of what the title said. I shot this video one time and it's performing pretty well. And about a month later, one of my friends sees it, and he posts it to social media, Facebook. Says, "hey everybody, what do you think about this? And there's my big old thumbnail, and there's my picture." It erupted on Facebook. That motherfucker, are you kidding? I mean, I got it, it was bad. I had every friend, everyone asking what I was playing at. Nobody actually watched the video. They just saw the title and the thumbnail. And there's one thing, one line you don't cross in Idaho. It's giving up hunting spots. Hunting and fishing is our fucking life. Our spots are our spots.

Within minutes you can be in the middle of a national forest. That's Idaho to me. And I shot that. I didn't give up hunting and fishing spots. What I talked about was in general, different mountain ranges, different gulches, how close it was to this national forest. If you live there, you're close to the Paper Company, which is cool because for $20 you can go by this pass and you get access to all the paper company land. I wasn't giving out coordinates, but it did not look that way. And I immediately took that video down and just owned up to it. "Hey guys, you're right. I can see how that looks. That was pretty fucked. Now, if you guys watch the video, you understand that I actually say I'm never going to give up a hunting spot. That's our life. But what I'm going to do is if you're moving here and you want to move to an area where you can be close to the National Forest, go hiking.".

Then Connor reaches out to me one day and goes, "dude, take a load of this shit, what should we do?" These people had made a Facebook group against us. I'm like, what?! They would post our videos in there and these people would just shred us. Call us every name under the sun, and we're ruined in Idaho. And then we find out who created the group. It was a dude who moved to Idaho like 7 years earlier. He was not even from Idaho. Connor also put a post in there and said, "I get your guys' frustration, but you have to realize that these people are moving here regardless. They're just trying to find out information. We're not forcing them. And you have a really good business, business that I've referred people to. I also understand that you just moved here seven years ago too." So Connor hit that dude right in his gut. That was the way that Connor responded and I loved it. We weren't going to go cause a war, but we were going to get the facts out there.

So when you start getting those negative comments, leave that shit. Ain't nobody in the world been hated more than us. I got more negative comments than every one of you put together. I've had Facebook groups against me, friends call me. I don't give a shit no more. I'm out for me. At the end of the day, I'm helping so many people and it feels amazing.

CHAPTER 16

Leaving Portland

I get asked about this a lot: How did I leave a city, a team and a YouTube channel my face was all over. It's just blasphemy. It's also kinda new in the real estate industry that someone would up and leave and expect to still get business from the previous city.

The craziest thing about it is that one time Jesse and I were approached about our Portland YouTube channel. A high-producing real estate team wanted to buy it off us. So Jesse went through all the legal processes. We weren't gonna sell it, we just wanted to know its valuation. By the way, Jesse's way better at telling this story than me. Still, he talked to the lawyer. Our lawyer had seen a lot of this kinda thing before. What happens is that person who owns the business is basically just selling a client list. He wanted to know if, given that our business was from YouTube, we knew exactly how many deals a potential buyer could expect. He also wanted to know if we handled all of the incoming calls and reach-outs or if there was a way to have someone else do it for us. Well, we did handle all inbound inquiries. The lawyer told us that if you can have other people answer the phone and close the deals, then you would have a 6x valuation on gross revenue. If you have to answer all the business and you're the face of the business, then it's basically worth nothing. So agents pack up and move to markets all the time, or they want to, but they fear it because they're the face of the business. Another reason why YouTube is one of the most incredible avenues to get business because when you lead with so much value, answer consumers' questions with content marketing, they're just dying to work with you. We've now learned through many, many transactions how to hand off deals. But at that time, we weren't quite sure. So I thought that was important to mention, because you actually do have flexibility to move even if you've built up a whole channel dedicated to one city.

When I was thinking about leaving, it was around July of 2020. But in March, April of 2020, we had made the move over to another realty company. And at first, this place seemed to be an absolute multi-level marketing pyramid scheme. I was so sick and tired of the agents there, I couldn't take them. But Jesse had done a bunch of homework at the time on different brokerages. We wanted to leave our previous spot because it was too small for us. We had outgrown the pond. We were really looking at scaling into these other markets. Not only that, but our previous brokerage was of the mind that we should really continue to focus on traditional real estate, telling us that the YouTube stuff is just a flash in the pan.

Jesse went insane on the research for three solid months before we moved. He went to every brokerage, took their tours, everything. His real estate coach at the time, Frank Driscoll, said that they should just sit down and have a talk. His coach had joined this new brokerage, and we ended up following suit. I remember now starting to notice that all these big influencers were going over to this new spot too. I couldn't get why. It had all the markings of a pyramid scheme.

Jesse actually got on the phone with the vice president and some higher ups who do tens of millions, hundreds of millions, billions of dollars annually in production with this place, eXp Realty. From that, he gleaned that you could partner with agents and teach them. In turn, you'd earn 2-3 different additional revenue streams on top of closing your deals. It's revenue share, not profit share. Now we would have the ability to teach these agents across the country for free, blow up their business, and we can earn additional revenue by doing so from the brokerage. Plus, now we can partner with agents anywhere in the world, and we're not held down by brick and mortar and franchise fees. That was Jesse's thinking. I was like, "these motherfuckers better just put me up." That's all I wanted. I didn't even get this revenue share thing. I was just thinking about these top influencers and getting on their podcasts. That was my whole thinking, 100%.

So we made that switch over to eXp Realty on March 1st, 2020 and within the first week I was on 10 of the biggest podcasts in the real estate world. It was amazing. I'd never felt anything like it. From the move, we had 10X growth, both in our real estate business and just the whole YouTube agent thing. Jesse's plan was to surround himself with the biggest and the baddest. He wanted to take us to the next level and to do it, he was gonna get in with these people.

Well now, under the eXp umbrella, they're trying to get us to go to that next level. The more revenue brought in, half of the revenue that goes into the company dollar (cap) now goes back to the agents in the form of Revenue Share. That's the whole point of the game. So one guy (who brought in billions in sales) said, "Jesse, you're the problem." You imagine telling Jesse that? Why is my business not growing and scaling? Because you're the problem, Jesse. What? Jesse's the most stone cold killin', real estate deal closin', driven human being I've ever seen. He's gotta close these deals. And yet we were stuck at 14 million. We just couldn't get past that because we had hit our ceiling. So this is when we started looking into bringing on buyer's agents and partners. We sat down with another agent who ran one of the most successful teams there with the highest paid buyer's agents. We asked him "what's your splits? What's your structure?" And he said, "you've got to take care of your agents. It's sickening in this world that we just force these agents to cold call and prospect and then they just get 25-50% of the deal. That's why it's a revolving door," he said,

"I wanted my agents to never leave me." He went on to explain that he has a kind of a sliding scale. So zero through 15 deals, he paid 30%. So a little bit more than a normal agent. After that, deals 15 through 30 would be 40%. Then, once you hit 40 deals, you go to 50% for life. It doesn't reset. But if an agent brings his own deal in, the team take is only 25%, and the agent gets 75%. So now not only do they get more favorable splits than any other agent out there, but they're more incentivized to go get their own business because they get a higher percentage.

Jesse always told me that he didn't want to just build this team, like a Keller model. That's what everybody does, it's a big old puff your chest out, 'I got a have a team who has the biggest team.' He was on the number one team when he got into real estate, and he hated it because he was the one bringing in all the business, he kicked the shit out of every other buyer's agent there. He was doing all of the prospecting, landing the deals, and he only made 50% on the buy side and 25% on the listing side. So he had pure hatred for the team model. His whole goal was to be able to bring up the business, bring in the business, and just hand it off to agents to close. Well, this YouTube thing kinda started happening, and we needed help. And this guy says to Jesse "you're the problem." So Jesse had to step out of production, and that means we had to train an agent.

A month or two before, one of the most epic humans I've ever worked with called to congratulate us on the YouTube success. She was the one that we did the elementary school thing with, but I'd also worked with her in the title business. I think she'd been in the title and escrow game for 20 or 30 years, and she'd been at the same company. She started with them as a customer service rep. She'd seen every real estate team, and decided we were different, so she wanted to join us. She had to quit that job. Had her son to support and her father was sick, but she ended up getting her real estate license, and she was our very first hire.

Jesse and I were in a spot where we had money rolling in. Compared to what I was making before, I was feeling like a rich bitch. I was killing it. But our new hire came on and immediately started taking some of these phone calls and Zoom calls with us. She was so nervous and anxious. But once she started to get warmed up, she was touring. And she was working like six or seven days a week. That's just how many clients we had. About four months into this, she sat with me and just started crying her eyes out. Firstly, Jesse's a really tough teacher. He's pushed me to limits to where I've just wanted to quit so many times, but it's always for a reason. Jesse's gonna push you to these limits to get the best out of you. So she's stressed out about that, and about trying to understand real estate and contracts. Plus she's touring seven days a week, and she ain't closing shit. She's crying, "I'm making no money. I'm literally a tour guide. I'm just doing all these tours, it's not freaking working. What do I do?" I told her that it was going to go any minute. People go through peaks and valleys, and this was just a valley but there was a peak just around the corner. By the next week, she started closing deals. In her first year, I think she closed 68 deals. When she was at our live event three months ago, I think she said she had 168 deals from YouTube in less than two years. So it came right around. A lot of people call me and say that their shit ain't working. "I say it's gonna happen, just stay consistent."

She is killing it. Her and Addy work really well together too. Addy is one of the most integral parts of this business, I talked about him earlier. He's on every Zoom call. So at this point, I'm 100% out of the Zoom calls. Jesse was kind of on some at the beginning, but with everything else going on he had to get off of them.

And that was the proof that we needed to, to show, hey, we don't have to answer these calls. Jesse actually botched a few deals where these people were just complete idiots and assholes; she took over and they ended up buying like five houses from her. So she took over the calls. So at this point, by the time I'm ready to go, I am just shooting the videos. Jesse is basically out of production, still helping with the team, but for the most part, he's out.

One day, I'm laying in bed with my wife and we were talking about moving. I was just over living in Portland. I Love Portland. It's the greatest thing that ever happened to me and my family and it's so much fun, but it wasn't truly who we were. So we were talking about the feelings we both had about it, and how we knew that it wasn't really *our* home. We also wanted to get back to our style of living. I remember saying to my wife "we should just sell this fucking house and just move to the coast, I can work from anywhere." She says, "Jackson, I'm not raising my kids in an Oregon coastal town. They're like the most drug infested places on earth." So yeah, the house is right on the Oregon coast, gorgeous, but if you cross over the highway, yeah, there's zero economy and it's just drug ridden. Then she said," Jackson, if you can move anywhere and live anywhere, take me back to Texas." For the past 10 years, that's all she ever talked about. She loved Texas. Now I did too; the culture, smokey barbecue, the people, the parties, and all the backyard events. I love entertaining and cooking, that's my shit. But after the two years I'd spent in Texas for my internship, I started to remember the heat. All I remember is how hot it was and that made me very hesitant. But I didn't have to work outside anymore. So I said "let's do it!" But now, oh boy, my guts started turning. How am I gonna tell my business partner I'm moving? He's gonna hate me. How am I gonna tell my team that I'm moving? I'm gonna crush their business, they're not gonna make any money. It's me on the video, I gotta be here.

Jesse was born and raised in Portland and he loves it there. Well, he loved it before the riots were going on. Now, I will defend Portland in that a lot of people from around the country thought the town was burning down. This was after seeing the riots on the news. But it was really just downtown. And Portland's real culture is based in its four quadrants.

With the exception of the Pearl district, downtown isn't reflective of Portland as a whole. Jesse lived in the Pearl, so he was right at the heart of it and could clearly see the rioting from his place. He was so pissed at our mayor that I thought he was gonna run for government and he still might.

Meanwhile, I had put off telling him about the move for weeks. Again, I don't know how to communicate. I was going to be letting him down, and letting everybody down. The business would obviously fail. But I already had a foot out the door, and my wife and I wanted to get to Texas. Right then, we were living in a three bed, two bathroom condo that's like 1,400 square feet. It had an estimate of $400,000. So I'm looking at $400,000 houses in Houston and seeing these 3500-square-footers. And they had a pool. That plus no state income tax, year-round warm weather, it was looking better and better by the day. So we're excited, we're like getting this going, but eventually had to break it to the team. Then Jesse calls me one night, freaking out, "Dude, they're attacking these buildings. I don't feel safe here. This place is a fucking shit hole. I'm so tired of this place. The government ain't doing shit, dude. I'm thinking about getting the hell out of here." And I perked up, "what? That's the craziest thing because my wife and I were just talking. We were thinking about moving to Texas." He continues, "I don't know why you're fucking still here, dude." What? Oh my God, it was the most pressure relieving thing on planet Earth. "Yeah, dude, you should get the hell out of here. Plus, Houston's an incredible area. We can go start a new channel." Hell. Yeah. His mind was all but made up on a move to Austin, Dallas or Phoenix. He was done. Again, I should have probably communicated earlier, I wouldn't have felt that stress for so long, but boom, my partner believed in me again and off we were going. I'm moving to Houston, Jesse went to Phoenix. And that's when we started launching more new channels.

Fortunately, I had just the person to close deals in Houston. I met Joe when he came through our course and then he went to one of our live boot camps. So Jesse sent him a message and he hops on a Zoom call with us. Joe's sitting there on his front porch and I'm just sitting there on the Zoom call feeling him out. I remember looking at his social media too and I was like, 'I don't know if he's my guy.' Then we get on this Zoom call and Jesse says, "how's your channel going?" Joe responds "oh, you know, I just haven't got to it yet. And you know, it's a lot of hard work. I got the camera, I'm gonna do it. I'm gonna get there." I tell him that I think I'm moving to Houston and I want to do a channel. Then he surprised me with blatant honesty, "I'll be honest with you guys, I'm never doing it, it's too hard. I hate video, but if you put a deal in front of me, I can close it." I was thrown back, he just spoke my language. I said, "Joe, you're the man for me."

So I found my business partner here in Joe and he's been an absolute rock star. I'll never forget when we moved here and we had to rent at first, because again, I didn't have two years of taxes that would show lenders that I was good for the money. So Joe and I are going to all these rentals and there's like a car out front. He's as confident as can be. He sees a car but just bangs on the door "boom, boom, boom, boom, boom," "realtor here". And I'm like, "damn, Joe." I'm standing out in the road because I'm so awkward. I told him there's somebody in the house, and I think it's so awkward. He comes back with "no, I don't give a shit. I scheduled this. It's our time. If they're in here they need to get out." I'm thinking, this man is the GOAT. So I had my business partner, Jesse ends up moving to Phoenix and ends up meeting a realtor and they're gonna do that channel together. Well, we learned quickly that now we're in some of the largest markets in the country and in our minds we're like, this is gonna be a gold mine, dude. Houston has 100,000 people moving to it a year. Phoenix is about the same. I'm now unstoppable in the real estate YouTube world. I'll just go outrank everybody. I'm gonna shoot these vlogs, these long-ass map videos. I can crush. And I'm coming off a mega high of Portland, killing it. North Idaho, fastest channel ever. And we got our asses kicked. The first 5 or 6 months of Houston, it was a flat line.

That's when I started understanding keyword research a little better. I found out that there were 350 million videos with the words 'Houston, Texas' in them. That's why it takes so long to break through. Like YouTube's trying to go through and find these videos and rank them. There was too much just other competition, not even real estate. I did have about seven or eight of my students here with *Living in Houston, Texas*, channels too.

Eventually, it finally broke through. You get that one video and it goes. And that's what I know now. So now I truly understand my data analytics. I'm trying to get my average view durations up on search the 6/7 minute mark. That's when I know I'm gonna start getting more recommended videos. And my suggested videos, I want an average of 10 to 11 minutes. That's my perfect recipe to just break through. Now in some markets it may take longer, some it won't, but if I can get to those numbers, those average view durations, it's gonna go. And Houston nailed that shit. It is now the fastest growing channel.

Joe wrote us a letter at the end of 2020. He'd been in real estate for 14 years. The most he'd ever made in commissions was 50 grand. He told me at one point he had a credit card with a $5,000 limit and for eight years he couldn't pay it off. And in 2021, he had over $500,000 in gross commissions. He told us that we literally 10x'd his business. He's remodeling a house with over $100,000 cash. He said that his whole life he has financed everything. Now he could afford a complete overhaul of his house and pay for it with cash.

This channel is an absolute rocket ship. It's hard as hell to break through these big markets, but when they go, they go. I was consistent as hell, and I shot long-ass videos. I studied my analytics and my drivers, and the Woodlands is the number one driver, so I hammered the shit out of those keywords. And Sugarland was, so I hammered those too. I kept 80% of my videos about Houston, and just took over the market.

Jesse's channel for the first eight months, flatline. So he said, "Jackson, just get your ass over here and shoot your videos." So I did. It is the first time I got to pack up my family and take them with me on a work trip. Like it was the most fucking special thing in the world. To be able to pay for my family to come, stay at a crazy cool hotel, have pool nights, go hiking, but I had to get my two days of work in. This is when I started my 20 videos in two days system, and it works.

I kind of failed to mention, I also at this point had my editor, so I'm not editing any videos anymore. I can't do that with all the other stuff going in. I found one on Fiverr. He was 25 bucks a video. I tried other Fiverr people before on different things, and I always went to the ones who had the most reviews. What I learned is, yeah, they'll do a good job, but it usually takes a little bit longer, and there's not the greatest communication. So I decided to try somebody who only had a couple reviews, but they're all five stars. To this day, he's still my number one guy. Every single video you've seen in the last three and a half years, no matter what the channel is, from channel junkies to all 11 other ones, 100% him. For Christmas, I sent him a $500 bonus. I also send cash on birthdays, holidays. He said that I've changed his whole family's life. I love this human being and we finally brought him onto the team full time.

So this is when I'm in Phoenix and Jesse's new business partner, she's going to shoot the videos with me. So she comes to pick me up. She's got a stack of papers, data, information, market, history. She's looking through all these notes and she's reading them and I'm just not paying attention. She's like, all right, so where do we start? I said, where's an area that's probably the farthest out that people really love and are moving to? She's like, well, probably North Scottsdale.

So she's like, all right, what kind of data do you need? I'm just ignoring her, I'm looking around. All I do is observe. Just looking around, looking around, looking around. I'm like, this is ugly. Then we get up to North Scottsdale and she shows me a neighborhood around the $500,000 mark. It's kind of a nicer neighborhood, but like a starter edition. I'm thinking, damn, 500,000 starter around Phoenix? I thought Phoenix was closer to $200,000 for houses.

Then we go to some $700,000 homes and they're tiny. I also notice that there's not a blade of grass within a thousand miles of this neighborhood. It's all lava rock and cacti. Bingo, there's my story. It's okay to disagree with areas, people want to know all aspects of a place. So she has all these notes and I tell her to get rid of that shit. So we're driving down the 101. She tells me that it was actually only finished in this area 5-10 years ago, and that's what made the whole North Scottsdale and DC Ranch regions popular. You can get out there quickly. And now all the tech companies are going out that way, so there's a lot of jobs and a strong economy. I ask her to pull over. So I hop out, and we're right by this mall. It's cool, you can take your family there. They have movie nights in the park, it was a good spot.

So I just stole everything she said, and added some of my own: *I was driving around North Scottsdale because everybody told me it was the greatest place to live for family, for kids. And I'm like, this is the ugliest place I've ever been. It made me not even want to move to Phoenix. There's not a blade of grass. I come from the Northwest. I want to see trees. I want to see grass. And I know that, with a nine, six, and two-year-old, I'm going to come home to a kid stuck in a cactus, and I ain't down for that.*

Thank God I learned about Gilbert and Chandler, where there's actually grass. So where these play areas are in North Scottsdale that are all gravel, you go down to Gilbert Chandler and it's all grass, and it's more small town living. So this is why you reach out to us, because you're gonna get told, or you're gonna read something that is perfect for you, and you ain't gonna feel it. You tell me two, three things you like, you don't like, and I'll be able to place you in the perfect spot.

So I went down to Phoenix and I shot my 20 videos in two days. That's where I learned a crazy organization process of labeling every single clip. I have this editor, he's from Afghanistan, he's never heard of DC Ranch, he's never heard of Phoenix. I had to start shooting videos of the map explaining where I was so that he knew it and he could create these map videos. I talk to my editor constantly. I'll be shooting, then say something like "editor, stop, stop, stop, okay. We just talked about DC Ranch, homes from 500 to 600,000. I'm gonna stick you out the window, this is all the B-roll for it. This is only a 30, 40 minute drive." Now I've got all my B-roll labeled. All the b-roll is mapped out in folders. If I ever say golf, there's an entire folder of just different golf shots. On that trip, I labeled every single clip, and that was when I started learning the process of handing these videos off to editors and having an amazing turnout. I don't even look at my videos anymore. I never have for the past two years. He's that fucking good, and I have prepared him. In fact, even with others, it's often not a shitty editor, it's just that people aren't mind readers. You have to show them exactly what you mean, that gives them the tools to do their part of the job the way you want it.

So, I'm living in Houston, Jesse was in Phoenix but now lives in Idaho. Portland, Phoenix, and Houston are all ripping. Now we're growing multiple channels.

CHAPTER 17

The More I Give, The Less You Do

Now, I bet you thought this book was going to be the direct playbook of exactly how to crush YouTube? I give all that shit away for free on YouTube, and I have for four years. I noticed at one point that the more I give and do for people, the less they were doing. And the message of this whole book is that doing things that you hate to do and that drive you nuts will ultimately lead you to massive crashes. It takes you away from the things that you enjoy and the things that actually bring you any money.

So in this chapter I'm going to discuss our very first marketing agency. At this point I have the system dialed and know exactly how to build a channel in about three minutes, what videos to shoot, and how to shoot the vlogs. I basically don't even need TubeBuddy anymore. At this point too, I'm also completely away from Keywords Everywhere, that shit was just leading me in directions that didn't work. TubeBuddy was life and it's what helped me debunk every myth by creating killer descriptions. Tagging Isn't really important, but just tracking my channels, tracking them every single day, split-testing thousands of thumbnails. I tweak one word and get a 2% better click-through rate, or tweak a different color and have a 1% lower click-through rate. Nowadays, I could go right into any market no matter what, and I'll dominate. We have created a YouTube for real estate system that is undeniably one of the best YouTube systems out there. I'm building channels all over, having crazy success.

So, when I came upon the realization that doing everything for people makes them do nothing, our course had been going for a while. But I also started realizing, well, I give it all away for free and I've had a dozen agents just take the free content and kill it. Then I started having the agents go, saying that they loved the videos, but they're not gonna watch 200 of them. So people were asking if we could do an A to Z playbook? And at the time I didn't, but then I built the course and it's the exact playbook A to Z. People were having crazy success from that. The cool thing about the course is that if you follow it and do it, it works. I've seen so many channels out there that have the exact green screen backgrounds that I put in the course, the exact copy paste templates. Yet 95% of people who bought the course never even opened it or went through it because they realized, oh shit, there's a lot to this and I gotta get on camera. They could build this channel out and follow the guides, but it was filling in the video. That's where people struggled. So I started just getting hounded by people asking for editors and secret systems.

Every single thing that we have built has been because the audience asked me for it. Well, Jesse wanted to build a massive business. The funny thing is when we started having discussions about building the done-for-you program, I was starting to think that the more we do and help, the less people are going to do. But I thought, if we were gonna do this, we truly had to get in there and help everybody. We've got to give them the video titles. We have to upload it for them. We have to do everything for them. All people have to do is turn on the camera, shoot the video, send it back to us. By this point, I've also had hundreds of consulting calls and coaching calls. And so what we did, and I didn't even know what this term meant, but we 'white labeled.' We had found this girl at the time and she had a killer marketing program, had the editors in place, everything that she presented to us was in diagrams and it was all amazing. And that's what we were gonna do. We were going to bring people in, but it wouldn't be my marketing agency. We were just white labeling with them. And the recipe would be: if you want to do one video a week, then it's a four video a month package, and we'd also offer an eight video package.

So we're deciding to go through with this and it's actually before I left Portland and before I moved to Houston. We started this thing, and it was just like the course. The 5% that did the two videos a week, had our team manage it, and do everything, worked wonders. Well, just look at Will and Eli in Denver, now they're some of the most special humans ever. And I am never gonna take credit for their success, ever. Those dudes were consistent. Those dudes figured it out. There was never a day of like, 'ah, we're not going to do this.' They just have done two videos a week, every single week. They did the work. Now they're out of that, and they do it themselves. They're millionaires, they're fucking millionaires just from their YouTube channel. Not including all the other business they do. And if you haven't yet, you need to go follow Eli Schmidt and Will Grimes. They spoke on our stage and they made the hair on my arms and neck stand up because of the way that they prepare their business, their buyers, their listings, and all the stuff that I don't have. But they were a prime example of people who went through the agency. And there were a couple others too. 97% of the people that went through there and paid a lot of money, didn't do the work. We White Labeled it, so we would let people know to reach out to that team for all problems. But everything came back to me. Every single day I'm putting out fires, I'm getting bitched at, I'm getting cussed out, I'm, mother fuck this, there are fights... I'm trying to put these fires out, yet the more that I'm doing for these people, the less they are doing. They're paying thousands and thousands of dollars and we're doing everything and we're sending them titles and we're building their channel, scheduling, uploading titles, text descriptions, thumbnails, metadata, and yet you can't turn a camera on and talk? And boy, let me hear some of the excuses that I heard.

I have poured my life into these systems. I have gone through the depths of hell of depression and debunking all of this stuff that doesn't work and if you just follow it, it freaking works. And you're going to sit on the other end of this email, cuss me out and demand your money back? Even after we did the work on our end.

Dealing with that took me away from what I loved doing, which was teaching real estate agents how to change their life by attracting their ideal clientele, never having to fucking cold call, door knock, or do anything like that again.

I'm shaking right now, because I'm reliving this. And so I got to a breaking point. Jesse wanted more people in this agency, and he's looking at the numbers of the business side of it. And I'm telling him that I'm getting bitched out on the daily. But then I eventually agreed to keep doing it. That was until the day that I snapped. I called Jesse and said he could have that part of the business "I don't want another fucking penny from it. I'm dealing with all these people every day, I hate YouTube for real estate." I'm sorry, but I also said, "I hate realtors, I hate them!" I didn't mean it, not for the good ones but some of them are so whiny.

So it took a little bit of time. And after a while, yes, Jesse came around too. It was just not viable. So I vowed to him that we'd replace it with something better, a similar product but just for business owners. But I didn't feel confident in that yet so I did it for free, for more than just real estate companies. I helped a golf company, a jet brokerage, I even helped a gal with her Rodan and Fields YouTube channel. I just told them that I wanted to learn how to do it, and I wasn't going to charge them anything. But I also started understanding that that wasn't my passion either. And so now I was lost. I didn't want to help real estate agents, I didn't want to help business owners.

Jesse started having these talks and I told him that all my desire to do this stuff was gone. I didn't even want to shoot real estate videos anymore. The only thing I wanted to do was to get up on stage and help people that way.

We'd continue to have a course out there because if people really want to change their life, they can do the work. I think we've sold over a thousand courses. I've never in a million years had one reach out of somebody saying the course sucked. It's either they don't say anything at all because they're overwhelmed and otherwise. But we have lots of people that go through it say, that's the best fucking course they've ever done.

I took so many courses back in the day. I spent thousands of dollars, went into debt and all of these courses had modules that were around two hours long. Who has time for that? It was also shit like 'go wrap your car,' 'get a thousand business cards and stand outside of Home Depot,' 'make sure you put out 400 million signs up,' and always 'have balloons.' All this shit to convert people, I couldn't do that. So I'm sure as hell not going to tell my students to do that, much less over the course of 2 hours per segment.

Our modules are 2-5 minutes long. In them, I'm showing you exactly how to go to Google and set up a YouTube account, discover the right keywords, build the descriptions–the whole book, A to Z. People who have gone through it and followed the course, they're the ones who have some of the most successful YouTube channels to this day. And I'm not trying to take credit for that. They put in the work.

As you know from this book, there have been plenty of times when I almost quit. Why? because I was doing stuff I didn't want to do. Now I'm starting to learn how to express my opinions. That hey, if something isn't working and it's taking me away from what actually brings me joy–which also makes me the most money–then let's stop doing it. Trader Joe's rule, 80-20.

I stopped doing videos for Portland. You can look on there, three month gaps, four month gaps. I stopped doing videos for Houston, two month gap, three month gap. I stopped doing videos for Channel Junkies. And the videos got shorter. And honestly, I'm sitting there and I'm teaching YouTube for real estate and I'm pissed at everybody. I've trained myself to look into the camera and act like I'm talking to somebody. And yet the person I'm talking to in that video, I'm frustrated at.

But the good news is I acknowledged it, talked about it with a business partner who accepted it. He may be the most incredible business minded human ever, but one thing that makes him great too is that he listens to me. And so when I told him I'm done, you can fucking have it, he listened and we pulled the rip cord. We pivoted. That's what led us down the path of doing boot camps. Some of you probably sat in those, for 199 bucks, I give them away. There are people selling 100 homes a year that came from the boot camp.

I will always remember going through those bootcamps and at the end of it my wife would say, "how'd you do?" She's the greatest supporter of all time. She always wants to make sure I'm doing good. The videos that people sent me, thanking me, are the absolute best. I needed to get back to teaching that and getting that passion.

If there's something in your business or life that you hate doing and it's taking you away from pleasure, stop it. You're going to feel amazing. And I'm looking in the camera right now and I'm reminding myself of that too. Don't ever forget that. Because when you relieve yourself from that and you remove yourself from people who bring you down, you end up making more money. You end up having so much more fun. And you're not an asshole at home, taking it out on your wife or kids.

So the more I was giving, the less they were doing. But at the same time, now I give 10x more. I have podcasts, blogs, a book, and YouTube videos. I give a lot of it away for free and I make you work a little bit harder for it. That is the shit that I love. I'm back, baby.

CHAPTER 18

The Traveling YouTuber

These days, in the real estate industry, I'm most known for having a shitload of YouTube channels all across the country. I don't have to answer the phone calls and we're selling homes everywhere. Once the travel started, damn I felt good. I was on cloud nine. I was done with this agency bullshit. Like Christopher Columbus, I'm doing something that nobody in the world has ever done. And I'm getting acknowledged for it.

So the very first trip, we locked down two partners. One was from Reno, Nevada, he actually went to my high school. And the other one was from Bozeman, Montana. At this point Seattle started ranking. It had been 300 days without a video, but it started just working. For some reason, something happened, and it started to blow up. So on January 8th, 2021, little over 10 months/300 days, we are starting to get all these phone calls of people wanting to actually buy in Seattle. It felt good to know that, even though I quit on it for basically a year, those videos always work.

As fortune would have it, one of my favorite homies from high school, Tova, had been living in Seattle. I told Jesse, "dude, she's a killer." She's smart, she was just awesome in high school, and she can close. We weren't gonna close these, so I called Tova, "hey, we got these YouTube leads, do you wanna take them and close them?" She agreed. For the first few leads, we jumped on the Zoom calls together. She blew me away. In that first call I took with Tova, she looks the client right in the eye and says, "look, I just want to prepare you. This market's crazy, it's expensive. On average, we're gonna make three offers and you're not gonna get that house. I just want you to be aware of that." Meanwhile, I'm in the back thinking 'oh my god.' The client let her know that he was glad she prepped them. Funnily enough, it made them so much more invested, you could see them scooching toward the screen a little closer and looking at her. They respected her. So we hand all those deals off. She's killing it and she starts shooting the videos.

I go to Bozeman. I do a back-to-back trip from Bozeman to Reno. 20 videos in two days for each spot. I'm freed up. I ain't gotta do nothing. I'm happy. I come back, get those videos edited by my Fiverr editor, and he just crushes it. I get all those videos uploaded, scheduled, and I'm loving life.

I was back in North Idaho, but really wanted to get down to Boise. That was one of the hottest markets. This gal ended up reaching out from Boise. Crazy enough, she reaches out and says she wanted to do it as well as partner with the eXp. So I head down there and meet her. Problem was, she would not say a word on video. I called Jesse, "we're fucked. I can't get a word, she's telling me these great stories, but every time I put the camera on her, she goes, oh no, no, no, I can't say that. I don't know if that's true." So I had to take what she'd told me and get on camera. I got nothing out of her.

She told me that the team lead over at her brokerage said he'd do some videos, and I'm like, *okay, whatever.* So I met him the next day. He's dressed to the nines, ripped, good looking dude. We get in his car, we start cruising, she's sitting in the back, and he and I just build this connection. He is hilarious and he's got stories of every single neighborhood. He's born and raised in the area. So, I was feeling a little less screwed at this point. He knocked it out of the park. We crushed it, we got those videos done, we made some sick-ass videos in Boise. He had been doing real estate for 15 or 20 years. He'd run multiple teams, upwards of 15 people. He explains that his whole business used to be cheap and now it's expensive. Over his career, he had closed hundreds of homes. But he never knew how to do the luxury sales. That all changed when the area shot up and he started getting calls, calls, calls.

In fact, he just called us the other day. He's signing $1.2 million contracts, new construction. He has about 11 buyers, most of them are in the million dollar range. And he says to us, "the best part is, I'm like a rock star to these people. I'm over here signing boobies."

I've said this in my podcast, but I still think that's the funniest thing I've ever heard.

That's something we get from helping people, all these different personalities and connections. If you look at the North Idaho channel, we have another competitor in there who's got 6,000 more views and a viral video. He's crushing it. I helped him when he was about 12 videos in. He said he was going to quit because he thought that everyone else was just thinking that he was copying us. I'm like, "dude, you got this, be you." He has now given over $50 million worth of referrals and he overtook our channel. He partnered with me at EXP.

That's what I do. I want to 10X you. Traveling from Seattle, Washington to the Florida Keys and everywhere in between, I know every market. I'm now coaching these agents and I can look at them and their market and I'm coaching them completely differently than I was before. This is why when I do my coaching and consulting, it's never about magic buttons and SEO and all that. I'm trying to coach you up to be yourself.

CHAPTER 19

Leverage & Delegation Are Key

As I had a very hard time delegating my video tasks, Jesse had a tough time letting go of the business tasks. Jesse and I now have 14 different virtual assistants doing every ounce of our business together so that we can focus on taking all of the businesses to the next level. It's crazy, but we had to start leaning on people. But I like hearing this from Mr. J Dau: Just blowing up super fast like yourself.

How are people doing it [gaining massive success] faster than ever before? It's because they're understanding leverage. And that's the thing, and you'll see it happen all the time, all of a sudden there's this shift in the mind. And also COVID was one of the most amazing things for almost everyone in this room, because what we all started realizing is that we didn't have to do it all, and we could become more dependent on technology. Everyone that says technology this, technology that. Well, quite honestly, unless you're using technology the right way and being effective with it, it doesn't really matter, right? So at the end *of the day, it's all about effectively using technology and virtual assistants, you know? And the greatest part about the virtual assistant model is that the cost is extremely low, right? If we could all hire, if we hired these people here in America and paid them top dollar, we would be spending 50 to $150,000 a year per position.*

These VAs are super great at what they do, they're even better than you are. So guess what? You think you can do it better but they can actually do it way better than you.

So the whole time we've been doing this, every time that we kind of offload something to a virtual assistant or another buyer's agent, team member, executive assistant, we grow substantially. Yet, why is it so damn difficult to do it? It's kind of like when I was a kid and I wanted to go build a skateboard ramp. I'd go into the garage, grab my dad's hammer, saw and shit, and I'd be kind of hacking away at stuff. He'd just come out, "get out of the way, I'll just do it." It's like that whole mentality of just, I'll do it. When we see people struggling doing something that we can do easily, we feel like we don't have time to teach them. We've leveraged VAs and especially me on my path of learning all this YouTube stuff where I did everything 100% myself.

Going all the way back to Seattle, Portland and early on in the YouTube channel, the YouTube Agents channel, I was doing 100% of everything. At that time I leveraged nothing. I was making no money. I thought I couldn't afford any of this stuff. The funny thing was, Jesse always said, "hey, can we get you an editor?" And I was like, nah, I'm good. I mean, guys, I invented this real estate vlog. I had the sickest intros to these beats, and you can see kind of the evolution of those as time went on, and that was my baby. So, when it came to finding an editor, that was probably one of the hardest things I had to give up. Yet, it was the most important thing that I ever gave up. It allowed me to get to even just doing this book today, and doing all the YouTube channels traveling. I'm not gonna lie, our editor is so much better at editing than me, it's crazy, and he knows my style so well. I mean, I barely have to explain anything anymore, I don't even look at any videos. Even if I ever just need something specially done, it's exactly the way I would do it, but better.

So we have to, in our business, understand that if we truly want to grow, growth comes from doing the things that we're the best at and everything else should be delegated. Now when I got into real estate, Jesse had always mentioned that he'd never do any of the paperwork. $400, $450 for transaction management, no brainer. So he kind of understood that leverage and he did come from corporate America. It'll be fascinating when I get his ass to do a book to talk about his mindset behind leverage and delegation because he's in the weeds every day with hundreds of agents, trying to help them take their business to the next level. It always comes down to delegation, finding partners, getting virtual assistants, and finding people who can do the creative too.

I don't want to get into any more real sob stories, but the only way that I think I can relate with you guys is to just tell the truth. So earlier this year, I had gotten to a point again, where I ran out of creative juice. I was spread pretty thin. Even though I didn't have to edit the videos or shoot the videos for any of these channels, I was taking the videos from the agent, giving it to my editor, and then getting that video back and uploading it. So I was still doing a lot of the work. And when you break down hourly costs, I spend 3-5 hours a day doing that, it's a task that's maybe five bucks an hour. So that's not where my time is most valuable. I also had my in-laws move in with us for a while. Love them to death. And I'm tighter with them than some of my own family. But when we had nine of us living in a house for 7 months, I got into a funk. I'm sure they did too. My office was my niece's bedroom. She's my homie, love her to death, but I couldn't get as much done.

Jesse and I went to a Sphere Rocket event where they leverage VAs. They basically headhunt and find you the perfect VA for you. Now, if you ever want more information on this, our free Facebook group, Channel Junkies YouTube for Real Estate, you can ask in there. We have links to schedule calls. But I'm not here to sell that, I'm just trying to talk about the art of delegation. We left that event pumped up. I was going to delegate everything. Jesse loves leverage, absolutely loves it. And then like a week later, I had a scheduled call with some virtual assistants. Jesse asks "hey, how'd your call go?" And I said, "I canceled it." A bit perplexed, he says, "really, why?" Feeling defeated, I say, "I don't even know what I could have VAs do for me. I don't know,

I just felt bad scheduling this call when I don't really know what I could have them do." It seems like a simple thing, not much to it. But I was pretty lost.

I had so many things going on. I wasn't shooting videos, it's just, I wanted to just get all this information out of my head. It was before our Walk and Talk podcast. I had visions of the book and that's really what I wanted to do. Yet, I was kind of halted on doing anything creative because I was doing all of this YouTube channel management.

So a day or two goes by and Jesse writes me an email. In it, he says:

I want to circle back to a conversation we briefly touched on before about you hiring a VA. I know you said that you don't have anything for them to do, but I think that there is a lot of value in a VA that can really help you with your time management and your calendar management and reminders. It's basically like having a personal assistant.

The reason I say this is because I feel I have to constantly remind you about things and send links and whatnot. I also see a lot of emails that start with, hey, sorry for the delayed response. Personally, I start to build resentment when I have to conduct basic tasks for other individuals or remind people to do their jobs. I don't wanna resent you. I wanna continue kicking ass and moving the ball down the field. And I wanna know that you are always going to be there and execute on your commitments and our commitments as a company.

Think about when you went on vacation and I sent you a note asking if you notified the group. I think I have to do that every time for you. Imagine your assistant knowing you're going to be gone and having already done that for you. And when I booked a sales event last week, you had to leave early. If there's a conflict with anything, we need to adjust so that we are both there.

Now we help a lot of people, and in the eyes of these people look to us and we need to be all-in 150% for things to work when it's time. *It's like hiring Clients & Community when we were struggling with our core sales. So I went out and found someone that could help and now it's popping. We could have kept going at it the way that we were, but it was very painful. But we made a shift and we're having exponential growth.*

Here's what I see a VA doing for you regarding your business. Meeting with you daily to go over your schedule, send you task lists for your items to do: Oversee your inbound emails, make sure you're responding in a timely manner, sending you reminders before meetings with links, post on your behalf inside your social media accounts, do your rescheduling if need be well in advance. Follow up with you to ensure things are done, make sure at least one video per week gets posted to the main channels, have a VA send reminders to the other agents about getting more videos going. The more you shoot, the more we make and anything else that you need.

It's basically $680 a month to make this happen. It's going to be like hiring all other VAs I have suggested. You will be thanking me for this one too.

Now, out of that whole email, the part where he said "I don't want to resent you" hit me the most. Now I was in a funk, and when he hit me with this email, I could have been down and oh poor me. I was like fuck yes. That's exactly what I need. I was so lost and so busy and just doing all of this work that I shouldn't be doing, that I didn't even know what I needed help with.

In the conversations I've had with thousands of agents, and Jesse's had even more, 99.9% of us agents, we don't know what we need help with, but right there was a massive list. Read this chapter again.

I'm a sticky note kind of guy. I will forget everything. Before any of this, I was a human who ran by a habitual schedule. I woke up at 4.30, I drove to work, I clocked in, and I left. If I clocked in one minute late, it was Union. If you leave one minute early, that was wrong. My whole life I've been told exactly where to be and how to be there, and I was never late. But now I'm an entrepreneur, my mind does not work in a sense of just remembering things. Just ask any of my family members about remembering birthdays. I can't, it just does not work in my brain.

I needed somebody who could manage Jackson Wilkey. I can do video, help others, speak on camera and stage, and to bring in real estate clients–and that's what I need to focus on. Everything else I didn't know I needed help with, I definitely needed help with. So that's how I met Mary. And some of you probably have been on the calls and she's right there. She saved my life.

Hiring a VA is a pretty cool process. I got to go through and interview 7 potential VAs and pick the one who fit best. Now, I'm not saying you must have a virtual assistant, everybody here doesn't need one. At the same time, it's pretty freaking amazing. Now my entire schedule is managed. Now she's on every single Zoom call. She clarifies everything that was said. Anything that I needed to remember is already in my calendar. Everything that any agent ever emails me, she's watching, she's monitoring, and if she has the link, she can send it before me, great. Every time I'm going on vacation, I'm letting her know, or traveling for work, whatever, and she's notifying groups. It's all done for me.

It's great now, but after I read that email, I knew I needed to talk to my J Dau. I went out into my truck, because my family was all around and I didn't want a blubber in front of them. And I called him and I could tell right away that he probably thought I was going to fight him. And I just opened up, "thank you so much, dude. I had no idea what I needed help with. I didn't. I was lost." With everything going on, I just opened up to him and I bawled my eyes out. Jesse and I have been through everything. You know what he was really mad at me about? That I didn't open up earlier.

It's the same reason that we brought Ryan Strong onto the channel junkies. The dude can do things that I've just never seen a human do and he does it faster than anybody. Websites, blogs, SEO, super human tasks, and the Channel Junkies and you guys get to reap all the benefits of that.

I want to give you guys some true insights on how to delegate effectively because I don't want to hear people say, *well, I got one, but they didn't do a good job.* You already heard what I told you earlier. That's a you problem. When handing off video to an editor, you have to make sure that you are doing the upfront work. If you're going to be sending clips to an editor, then you need to make sure that those clips are labeled. What I love to do is I'll wave my arms in front of the camera and say, "hey editor, I got some B-roll in a folder. When I mention going to the park, there's some footage of that park I want you to drop in there. I'm going to be talking about [x number of] areas today. Make sure that you're making maps and pointing to those areas." They edit that whole part out of the video, but it makes it way easier for them. Anytime that I'm talking and I remember anything, I say "stop, editor, stop, stop, stop, stop," "Hey, I have some B-roll for that," or "hey, make sure you put this graph in." So I will talk to him, talk to him, talk to him, talk to him.

I've already talked about this, but it's that important. Make sure that you are explaining *all* of your content. And over time, you will find your editor like mine. He's probably done 1,500 videos for me and he now knows me. I don't have to explain anything anymore, nothing. He just gets it. We've invented this system together to where he keeps all of my b-roll saved in his editor. I didn't even know this until like two months ago. Whenever I mention anything, he can type into his editor that city or element and it pulls up specific clips that he knows he likes. It then just drops it in there. Like I said, he's so much better than I am.

By paying him 25 bucks a video, if I went back and looked, I probably should have for the book, but I would imagine I've probably spent around $15,000, maybe a little bit more. We've sold 450+ homes from these videos, and YouTube doesn't cost me a dime. In totality, we've done, I believe, almost 255 million in sales volume. So I think a $15,000 investment is well worth it. Now, going back, I would have paid that $20,000 loan I got from my friend to have an editor come in, so that I could concentrate on knocking videos out. If I would have spent $10,000 a month getting this YouTube thing going, just knowing how quickly it could have got me out of debt, building a brand and a legacy forever.

We look at upfront costs and we're like, "nope, I'm gonna pinch the pennies. I'm gonna do it myself." And it's the hardest thing to do and I'm admitting to you that even I struggled with it. But delegating is the most amazing feeling ever. Just like if I've had people not start their YouTube channel because their channel art holds them up. Trust me, there's nothing that you guys can say that I haven't coached through or helped somebody with. Channel art? Go to Fiverr, type in YouTube channel art. You'll find somebody who will do it for $10. Give them your picture, your logo, show them a couple that you like and boom, done. I've done it numerous times. Sometimes, I would edit a video, I got so good that I could do a vlog in maybe an hour and a half. Then I would spend three hours on the thumbnail just trying to perfect it. Now I go back and look at some of those, I'm like, yikes, those are terrible.

Every single thumbnail you see on every channel I got right now has been completely redone. So all of those hours and hours and hours probably add up to weeks and months of my life I'll never get back. I pay $2 a thumbnail right now and they are the most impressive, gorgeous thumbnails ever.

I also have a team of virtual assistants now who obviously do all my YouTube management. They're editing all of my videos. I still have my original Fiverr editor for all of my real estate YouTube stuff. He just knows me like the back of my hand. He's basically my main editor. I have another virtual assistant team who does all the Channel Junkie editing. They edit all the videos, write the title tag descriptions, upload, all of it.

Now my virtual or my executive assistant, the one that I got after Jesse got in my ass (and thank God he did), she does all my management. But I also had some ideas of starting to write blogs. I'm terrible at writing, but I just want to get all of this information out there. I love giving out information about YouTube for real estate. So I started writing blogs for channeljunkies.com. And then Ryan Strong, who's a genius, created me a blog template. He taught Mary, my assistant, how to upload and geotag, and all this crazy backlinking... He's going to laugh because I basically don't know any, and I don't want to learn any website stuff. And he already mastered it, so why not just bring that partner on? Jesse and I gave him a third of the business. Let's take this to the next level, it's 10X, right?

So Jesse and I built this thing for two plus years and we give a third of it away instantly. And guess what? He did more work in two weeks than either of us did in two years. Everything we were talking about and trying to get done; he knew it and he knows how to teach it.

Leverage and delegation, it will free you up and it will be the best thing that you ever do in your life. So I hope by reading this, you're going to at least accept it and realize that you can do this. It's on you to train this person up. Give them 1-4 weeks to figure you out. Because once they do figure it out, they're 10 times better than you, trust me.

So if you want to get better at leverage and delegation, like we mentioned, we have some resources that we use. You can go check them out in the free Facebook group, Channel Junkies. And I would love you to say, "you know what? I heard you talk about it in the book."

CHAPTER 20

Storytelling Mastery

I love incorporating stories, this whole book has been in story form, and it is the greatest way to communicate ever. People that you resonate with, the reason you do is because they've told some kind of story. If you watch any good YouTube video of somebody selling products or teaching you how to do something, if they have a good story up front, most people are sticking around to hear it.

Telling stories aligns you with your ideal clients. It took me so long to figure it out. And the worst part about that is, I went to college for it. I went to North Idaho College, right out of high school, played college basketball, and then went on to do a bachelor's in communications. Why? Because I was an athlete. I just wanted to play. Someone told me to just go into communications because it's the easiest. 'Perfect', I thought, 'I like that shit.'

That degree, even though I never planned to use it, taught me so many things that I wouldn't in a million years have thought I'd use. Part of the degree program was to do an apprenticeship. I went and worked for the local radio, *K-102 Country*. I love me some old-school country and I was ripping on that. Because of this, I started getting more confidence in announcing. Even to this day, my number one goal is getting on stage. I still get bubble guts when I do go up. It's getting easier, but it still rocks me. So, I went to college for communications and I'll never forget one of the tasks that we had to do in this one class. Our teacher would make us get up in front of the class. For 99.9% of people, their number one fear is public speaking. I know because even though I enjoy it, that shit still scares me sometimes. The whole goal in this class was who could talk the longest. You could talk about anything that you wanted. So this was not like, go write an essay and then speak about it. This was talk about anything in the entire world. The rules were that you could not say 'um', and you couldn't pause for more than three seconds. Soon as you do that, you're done. What did I choose? Hunting and fishing stories. Because you know hunting and fishing folks are the biggest storytelling people of all time. So, plenty of subject matter to work with while I tried to avoid the word 'um.' So I'm telling stories in this class and I can go for quite a while. But the most interesting thing happened after the class. When we were all done, the class members were closer, they understood each other more. When we were forced to talk about things and it's not scripted, it brought us all closer together.

It doesn't matter what the story is. If you tell stories, it keeps people's attention for a long time during and long after you've finished telling it. When they're telling it, you're dying to know the ending. When a trigger word or scenario reminds you of it, you recall at least parts of it all over again. Storytelling is some powerful shit.

The reason I'm going into this depth about storytelling is because when I got into real estate, you heard the first few chapters, I did none of this. All that college, all that training, and I threw it out the window and listened to other agents. I copied and emulated what I saw and I never told a story. Thus, my videos sucked and I never got business from those early ones.

Another thing I learned to do in college was bullet pointing. When I started out, I was scripting and writing paragraphs. I would study a paragraph and have a bullet point for it so that I could try to nail the factual data such as numbers, streets, dates, locations. Back then, I was so rigid that if I messed up one number in a median home price, I would have to go back, edit that video, and reshoot it. That'd always add at least an hour to my day. It takes so much time. Now I mess up street names, I've messed up lake names, I've mispronounced cities. I don't give a shit because I know people moving in, and they have no idea what I'm talking about. But we hold ourselves to this standard where everything has to be perfect. And yet, it's the stories that everybody wants to know. Here's one I had on a recent Living in Houston video:

Grew up my whole life in one area and I never left. So now I'm like, oh my gosh, people live outside of North Idaho. I can't believe it. So we like to travel around, meet people. You'll never find anything like the people down here in Texas. One of my jobs, you know, 10 plus years ago when I was building power lines, I was a journeyman lineman for a decade. I traveled 17 different states working power lines. And every time we worked these southern states, these people would do anything for us. They would lose their homes in tornadoes. They would lose their homes in hurricanes and they were always asking us if we needed anything. Like, I could not believe that. Went up to the Northeast–sorry New Yorkers–they were cussing me out because I didn't fix their power yet. They were chewing my ass because I haven't done something yet and it's just like, it was so different and I'm not just picking on Northeast, that's kind of everywhere, but this Southern hospitality down here is the number one reason it drew us back.

I love entertaining, I love going out and having neighbors invite you to barbecues and pool parties and there's just so many nice people here that are doing that and will do anything for you. They are the most accepting. In fact, my family from Utah just moved here as well. The kids were nervous, about starting at a new school; one in elementary, one in middle school. Both of them came back and said, "oh my gosh, the people here, the kids here are so nice. They all asked me, 'hey, can you come sit with us at lunch?'" It was just so warming, you know, to hear that. So my kids have said the same thing. That Southern hospitality is something that they're adapting to and adopting into their vocabulary, 'yes sir', 'yes ma'am', and we just absolutely love that. So those are the main reasons we moved here.

Again, comment down below the number one reason you're moving here and if any of those are things that you're gonna like. But that's what we do, we help place you in the right spot. The biggest problem with moving, relocating here to Texas is it's massive. Moving to the wrong area can make it not as enjoyable. So when you reach out, we answer just all of your questions. We ask a lot of questions, figure out why you're moving, what you like, what you don't like, and that way we can place you in the right spot. But the only way that we can do that is, you gotta reach out to us. You gotta give us a call, shoot us a text, send us an email. Days, nights, weekends, we got your back when moving to Houston, Texas. And until the next video, guys, we'll catch you later.

And so when I started out, I was scripting. I would be reading these things and they were very monotone. I've had agents say, "Jackson, will you take a look at my channel?" I look and their eyes are going back and forth, back and forth and they're reading my lines. It's often my exact intro and they take it because they think that it's the only way. They watch me and they're like, 'well it works for Jackson.' Then they just read my lines. *Hi, in this video we're gonna talk about the pros and cons of living in Houston, Texas. You're never gonna guess how hot it gets here and we're gonna talk about drinking brewskis. So stay tuned.* It's like, come on man. Tell your own story, be you. You're not gonna attract anybody and you're definitely not going to attract the people that you jam with unless you are yourself. Yes, we provide templates and tell train people how to talk, but more important than that will ever be is you being yourself.

When we go with factual information in history, nobody cares about it. It's also when we are the hardest on ourselves because we try to memorize it all. And when we memorize, it comes across as inauthentic. We watch social media videos, we watch YouTube videos, we watch all of this stuff, and the ones that we see (because they're ranking) are usually the most raw, uncut, unedited videos. And trust me, when people are moving, relocating to your city, they're interested in all of it, as long as it's not factual data. Now, I don't mind if you throw in some 'you're gonna be looking at about $600-700k. Like, yes, that's okay. But what does that $600-700k get the buyer?

During our early vlogs, when I was shooting these videos that I was being taught to do, I was not being myself. But when I inevitably started understanding that people were searching these cities and suburbs and I had myself moved to Portland, Oregon and were *dying* to know this information, I started loosening up a little bit. And once we started being ourselves, we got a couple comments from people saying that they loved our videos. With that, we started getting a little bit more confident. We started being ourselves more.

Once we started being ourselves and telling these stories, people were eating it up and the average viewer durations were just starting to increase and increase. Which, if you remember from earlier on in this book, is one of the top ranking factors. Viewer duration is everything.

There was this one girl who called me up and she was struggling. She was doing all this factual information. I told her that she needed to be herself. She told me that she knew, she'd watched my videos about hunting and fishing. "That's me," she said, "I wear cowgirl boots, I turkey hunt with my dad, I go bass fishing on this lake." I wanted so badly for her to just let go and open up about all that. She's like, "nope, ain't doing it." For the longest time, I could not get her to do it. But she finally did. Before that, she had zero reach-outs, she never got any business. When she started talking about being country girl and loving being a country girl and hunting and fishing with her dad; that's when shit popped. She called me up, "oh my God, I'm closing a $1.2 million, this is insane to me, $1.2 million." Now? She's working with million dollar luxury home buyers.

A guy in Houston is closing $8 million ranch deals and $3 million land development deals by just simply talking about land and ranch in Texas. He called me one day and said, "Jackson, I can't believe this. I'm driving all over the most beautiful parts of Texas. I'm at $15 million ranches with multi-millionaires and they love me. We're driving around on my side-by-side. I'm wearing my cowboy hat and my cowboy boots, and I'm eating supper under the stars next to the most gorgeous ranch I've ever seen." He found his passion, what he loved to talk about. He wore his own clothes, not something that corporate America picked out for him. And when he talked about what he loved, incorporated his stories, that made people trust him, and that made people reach out.

I will say that with these stories, you've got to make sure that you're bullet pointing. I still do this to this day. Now, a lot of times I look at a video title, I turn the frickin' camera on, and I roll. Just like this book, I never planned out a chapter. Wherever I left off, I knew exactly where I needed to start next, and then I can just sit here and I can tell you stories. This whole book, I'm basically staring at the wall or looking at myself and I am just talking because I am telling stories. But I do, if I look down, I have about nine bullet points right here. One says college communication. One says tell stories, hunt, fish, best storytellers. There's the Idaho one. These are just my bullet points and yet I'm able to go for a good 30 minutes because each one of these bullet points reminds me of the story I want to tell. Hopefully, it'll help you too. So your two to three words are just starting your story. That's the way that you need to look at it.

When I do my list videos, 'Top 9', 'Top 15', whatever it is, I will just have 1-3 words, or I'll have just the city. And then when I see that city name, all I'm gonna do is tell the story of what I've done in that area and who I've helped to move there. They're just triggers to help you along your way. Not structured, monotone script, but little reminders of where you wanted to go. The things you thought about when you hit your creative peak for the day, week, or month.

So, when I do these videos about cities, suburbs, and areas, I have that city written down. And what I'm going to do is give you stories about that area. What I used to do, and what 99% of the agents that I see do, is this: Let's say you wrote down Spirit Lake, Idaho. Now, anybody not from North Idaho, you have no idea what I'm talking about, correct? So I need to paint this picture of what Spirit Lake, Idaho is. This first example is the real estate way of doing it.

Spirit Lake, Idaho is 15 minutes directly north of Coeur d'Alene, Idaho. The median home price is right around $473,000. There are a multitude of different styles of living. Now, there is some new construction and you will find houses starting at around $400 to $500,000. There are also properties where you can get maybe one acre or five acres, and it's really depending on the home. You can get into some of those median home prices around 600,000. You have a grocery store called Miller's, and off of Highway 54 is a school, and this school is K through 12. So all the kids will be going together, which is kind of cute because they'll go to the same school the whole time. Spirit Lake was founded back in 1910, right next to the actual lake, which is Spirit Lake.

All right, enough of that shit. So that doesn't give you any kind of insight on Spirit Lake at all. That's a fucking plastic-ass way of explaining an area where someone is looking to move to and/or looking to move their entire family to.

So, this is how I would describe it now:

Spirit Lake is about 15 miles north of Coeur d'Alene. It's about a 30-40 minute drive and it's gonna be in farm country. You're surrounded 360 degrees by mountains. If coming to an area, getting that acreage, that space, is a goal of yours, Spirit Lake's an area that you want to look at.

Now, there are differences in North Idaho of getting two acres here versus there. But, Spirit Lake is an area where you're gonna be able to stretch your budget the most. It wasn't even until eight years ago, that Spirit Lake was even a thing. I had friends growing up there. There's an elementary school that's K through 12. Which is kinda weird, like I had buddies who went there and they're like seniors in high school and there are kindergartners there. But it's a good school and that's really what you have.

They have a downtown scene that's like three bars. You go down, hit up the Linker Logger. Dude, oh my God, it's epic. If you're here in June for Father's Day, you gotta head down there. They have lawnmower races down there and I'm not shittin' you. They literally line up the streets with old-ass men on these lawn mowers with just crazy, some of them are like caskets, some of them are like the Dukes of Hazard charger and they go 40 miles an hour up and down this street. And to start the event off, this dude rolls out, he's the size of Shaq, he's got a double barrel 10 gauge shotgun. He goes out to the middle. Some lady with a terrible voice sings the national anthem. And then he shoots this 10 gauge up into the air with a blank. And the party starts and you can drink tall boys out in the street.

Like, you guys have to realize when you're coming to Idaho, like Idaho's not changed, it's gorgeous. Top destination. You see the downtown Coeur d'Alene, the lakes, the tourists. But you get into some of these cities, it's a little bit behind the times. And that is Spirit Lake. That's why I love it. That's why my friends live in Spirit Lake. I actually have buddies who live there. You can get two acres, five acres. A couple of them have five acres. They have their giant barn too. They have some animals. Their kids love growing up there. They have motorcycle tracks. I actually take the kiddos out there with the four-wheelers, the motorcycles; we're jumping, hanging out. Me and the dads are kicking it in the shop, swapping hunting stories and drinking some beers and that's just life out there.

It's a little bit slower. You have Paper Company all around you, for $20 you get this pass and they gate it off so you cannot go up there if you don't have this pass. So you can hunt, you can fish; you will literally see four-wheelers, side-by-side razors just driving the streets. It's legal.

So that's one thing, if you're like, 'okay, I want North Idaho, I want my acreage, I want my space a little bit quieter', Spirit Lake's an area that you're gonna want to look. The things you need to know about Spirit Lake, that nobody moving here has any clue about, is if you are around that area, you are in a snowbelt. So if it snows seven inches in Coeur d'Alene, which is really nothing, you're gonna get 12 to 14 inches in Spirit Lake. It's gonna dump, okay? So you're really going to need some snow equipment. Your little shovel ain't gonna do shit. You've got to be able to throw that snow away.

I've worked power lines in this area, had to hike to people's backyards. I've built every power line there. I know every street, every house. Sometimes there's four or five feet of snow there, and if you just shovel it, well, you're gonna be buried in no time at all.

The other thing about the soil up there, because we were digging power lines, we had giant backhoes and they would hit these rocks the size of a Dodge Neon. You've got to have equipment if you're going to be maintaining this property. But that's what people love up there.

So now, to you book readers, which one of those are you following along with? Which one of those do you think you're going to watch longer? Which one of those gives you a better idea of whether that area fits you or not? Does it start sparking memories and things that you've done or are you, like, *get me the hell away from that redneck ass town*? At least you know, right? But by giving you information about the market and median home prices, you don't get that feeling. This is why that our North Idaho channel blew up so fast: 74 days, 1,000 subscribers, $14 million deals closed, people frantically calling us–only wanting to work with us. For once I got to wear the hat of being the local and I knocked that shit out of the park. This is how you need to realize you have to be on your videos, okay? Now, I'm not saying you gotta be me, you gotta be that kind of emphatic.

You just have to tell stories about an area. What have you done there with your kids? What have you done there by yourself? What have you done in that area with your friends? And why do you not like it if you don't choose to live there? Because that's going to help somebody move there, or not move there.

I want to try to get y'all away from scripting. Also, don't forget where you came from. Just like when I was a journeyman lineman. When you start out, you're a grunt. A grunt is a groundsman. And you do all the dirty work and clean everything up. Then if you're lucky enough, you get to become an ape, which is an apprentice. And then you're just basically one step higher than dog shit, right? You're dog shit, but it means that you're a little bit less smelly than dog shit, and then you become the JY, the journeyman, and then there's general foreman. But you're taught as a journeyman, don't ever forget where you came from. At one point, you were that grunt. And you're gonna rely on that grunt someday when you're topped out as the journeyman lineman. They're going to be there to protect you and help you go home to your family, because working with 35,000 volts of electricity is dangerous. So you better train him up right. But you also better not forget where you came from because stories are life.

Even so, there are some stories that you can't allow to define you. Nothing hit me harder than this day when Ryan Strong, who partnered with us, he said, "Jackson, I know there are a lot of agents asking for your help, and I think we can help them. I want to be able to help them with their videos, video titles, and editing." I stopped him right there and said, "hell no,

Ryan, ain't doing it." I said, "I will never help agents by doing that again. I've already gone down this road. I get blamed for everything. I just want to teach it all for free." He said, "Jackson, I know, but you have to realize that you're kind of a specimen. For you to just get eight video titles, turn the camera on and go; I can't do that." I was looking at him like, "dude, your channel's exploded. You're already out of production in two years. You have to be crushing these videos."But he persisted "no, dude, I still to this day, I have to organize everything. I have to plan everything. I have to have my scripts." I was kinda shocked at this, "really?" He goes, "yeah, I know you're against scripts, but I've figured out a way that I can incorporate these scripts into micro segments, 45 seconds to 90 seconds, and it can help me to create these 12-18 minute videos and everything is lined out." At this news, I'm thinking "no shit?!" But I still told him that I'd already been down this path and I'm not gonna help. I love helping agents and I want more and more and more people to do this, but I did not want to go there again. I said to him "the more I give, the less they do." His response was, "what was one of the biggest things that held people back?" I mean, I gave them the video title. All they had to do is shoot the video. Ryan's still on the train of thought that he had thought out very well, "that's the problem, right?" He continued "you look at a video title, what the hell do you say? That's my biggest issue I had."

I have a brain that just says, 'all right, I'm just gonna shoot this stuff, get it out, I don't care about the edits.' Now I'm just going, going, going, going. I'm gonna go ahead and do this. But when he showed me that system, I was blown away. And now? He's been helping agents by jumping on a call. He gives them the video title, and then he has the conversations with you. He actually gets you to tell him the story, writes it down in 10 different segments, hands it back to you, and now you get to just relay those 10 stories that you told him. It's a pretty incredible process.

Now, it would not be Jackson Wilkey to sit here and just sell you on shit, but the reason we build these things out is because I get dozens of reach-outs every day for help. So yes, I have 100+ videos on the Channel Junkies for free. I go live every Wednesday, answering every single question. I write blogs, I do podcasts, I now have a book. I've done it for three years and I'm gonna continue giving it away for free. You never ever, ever have to spend a dime. But because people asked, I built a course. Because I saw 95% of people bought the course and didn't go through it, that affected me more than anything. Dude, I put my life and soul into that course. It's the exact recipe. 95% of people didn't even go through it? So that's the system that Jesse and I built. I said, I wanna help more people, and I know what the problem is. They have the course, but they're getting held up at just creating a new email address or creating that channel art or understanding analytics and data. So they don't even get to the video part because they're overwhelmed. So what we're doing is helping agents and meeting them where they are with the agency. The only way it's going to work is if people show up. I'm going to tell them which videos to shoot and I'm gonna shoot the videos in front of them. I'm gonna teach them exactly how to shoot them, what to say, what to do.

When Ryan explained that people need help with their videos, that's when we built *Scale Plus*. Now if you ever want to look at any of these, just go to channeljunkies.com. Ryan built the most beautiful website of all time. It's all there. And if you just want it all free, go to the **Channel Junkies YouTube channel**. Hundreds of videos, constantly updating. I've had dozens of agents take my free stuff and change their lives. That's the greatest thing in the world. That's why I did it. But if you need that extra help, just check everything out at channeljunkies.com.

The ball is (always) in your court.

Made in the USA
Middletown, DE
10 February 2024

49483319R00150